The Abingdon Religious Education Texts
David G. Downey, General Editor

COLLEGE SERIES   GEORGE HERBERT BETTS, Editor

WHAT MAY I BELIEVE?

BY

EDMUND DAVISON SOPER

THE ABINGDON PRESS
NEW YORK   CINCINNATI

Copyright, 1927, by

, EDMUND DAVISON SOPER

Printed in the United States of America

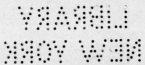

TO
MY . WIFE

CONTENTS

PREFACE

THE studies which comprise this book were first given before a class composed for the most part of students in Northwestern University. The purpose of the writer has not been to add to the number of systematic theologies. A much more modest aim has been his. He has found many during recent years—students, ministers, and members of churches—who are troubled and confused over questions of Christian doctrine. They were in trouble and did not know the way out. It was to meet, or help meet, that need that these studies were prepared.

Many things are omitted which should be included in a longer and more systematic treatise. The aim here has been to strike directly at the points where the problems were felt to be pressing, irrespective of many items which are closely related with those which have been chosen for treatment. It is very evident that anyone else essaying the same task would have chosen differently—but that is inevitable. The writer merely offers what has seemed important to him, hoping it may meet the needs of a wider constituency than he has been able to reach in a more personal way.

Many issues have been touched upon on which there is not only difference of opinion, but around which there has raged and is raging strenuous controversy. The theory on which these pages are written is that the only way progress can be made is for those who have convictions to speak out clearly and firmly without fear and without favor, provided—and this is of

7

great importance—the love of God is in their hearts and that they are willing to learn as well as to instruct. Nothing is to be gained in these days by attempting to conceal the issues in religious discussion. What men and women desire is candor without intolerance and frank statement without rancor.

It would be impossible to give credit to all to whom it is due. A few names appear in the text, but these are only a small fraction of the number of those whose works have contributed directly to these pages. It has been thought wise in a work like this not to encumber the pages with too numerous footnotes. But besides those whose names might easily have been given is that number whose influence has become so much a part of the warp and woof of one's everyday theological and devotional thinking that it would be impossible to list them. But to them as to others the author expresses his deep gratitude.

Duke University,
　　　Durham, North Carolina.　　　　E. D. S.

CHAPTER I

HOW MAY I KNOW THERE IS A GOD?

EVERYWHERE men believe in some power or powers which control their fortunes and destiny. Because this belief is well-nigh universal it has been thought that it renders belief in God certain. What is held to be true at all times and in every place and by everybody (*quod semper, quod ubique et quod omnibus*) ought to have sufficient weight to banish all doubt.

The argument may sound plausible, but can it bear the weight which it is made to carry? When the belief in higher powers is examined, instead of finding a uniform conception everywhere we discover the greatest variety of objects which are worshiped. It is exceedingly difficult to bring order out of the confused array. Men worship animals, plants, stones, mountains, water, fire, human beings—dead or alive—and the heavenly bodies. There are family, clan, and national gods. The religions of the more cultured peoples have highly developed gods, frequently arranged in hierarchies. The Jews worship Jehovah, Mohammedans Allah, and Christians the Father who was revealed by Jesus Christ. About all, then, that the universal diffusion of the belief in some higher power shows is that man has an inalienable tendency to believe in some agency higher than himself on whom he is dependent. But in no sense does it touch the particular question before us, How may I know that the God or the kind of God in whom we have been taught to believe really exists?

Another use may be made of the long list of powers or gods in whom men believe. When these gods, and the ideas connected with them, are studied in their relations with one another, it becomes quite evident that there has been a development. The needs of men have enlarged, and with that change there has been a corresponding change in the kind of powers or gods which are looked upon to bring the desired satisfaction. The refining process has been at work to make the idea suit the advancing moral and spiritual needs of men. What we are likely to say from this viewpoint is that the monotheism we have now reached is the final stage, that the God we worship cannot be superseded. There are those, however, who cannot accept this conclusion; they claim that we must eventually discard the idea of God just as we have discarded many other hoary ideas. Because a belief is old and has had a useful and honorable history is no reason why we may be confident that it will or ought to persist. Men believed in a flat earth at the center of the universe from the time they began to think about the earth at all (with the exception of a few Greek thinkers) until a few centuries ago, but we do not hold such a theory to-day. It would be an impossibility now with what we know of the sphere on which we live and its relation to our solar system and to the other systems in the expanse of the heavens. Is there any good reason for clinging to the conviction that there is a God? If there be development in the God-idea and we have been able to discover it, may it not happen that, as we have turned aside from so many other outworn ideas, we shall in due time discard this and be compelled to admit that there is no God after all?

The claim is made by those who deny the existence of God that we live in an age of science and that science cannot find God. It is an age of the telescope, the microscope, and the test tube, but these give no evidence that there is anywhere in the universe a being who corresponds to our description of God. Not only is this true but they say that the universe runs on irrespective of worship and prayer, without the slightest indication that a beneficent Father is at the helm guiding the course of events in any way. They account for the belief men have held about God by declaring that men imagined there was a God because they wanted a God, and then claimed that the God they had imagined and placed out there in their spirit world was an objective fact. Man has his hopes and fears and aspirations and these cause him to feel the need of some power stronger and wiser than himself who can be counted upon to stand by him in his weakness and fear—but it is all a mistake. In a world which is conducted not haphazard at the will of some more or less human and capricious god but in strict obedience to fixed laws there is no place for God even if we feel the need of one. Sooner or later we shall have to get rid of this burdensome old belief and accommodate ourselves to the actual world in which we live.

In dealing with such a theory we should, in the first place, express our deep satisfaction that science is coming to its own and that we are able to learn most valuable lessons from it. It is a great boon for anyone to know that he lives in a universe in which things do not just happen, but are subject to laws

which are uniform and dependable. Instead of living
in a world like that of the savage, in which anything
might be or become anything else, and in which he is
constantly in dread of some mysterious and irrespon-
sible happening which is likely at any time to over-
take him, we find ourselves more and more at home
in the world in which we live. Its forces are being
harnessed to our needs and show themselves amenable
to our will. We are so sure of the uniformity of its
operations that we act upon it and are not disap-
pointed. So much a part of our daily life have these
experiences become that we almost take them for
granted. Yet it is well for us to realize now and then
how different our outlook is from that of the generations which lived in a world on which they could not
depend, but which was capricious and uncertain and
misleading. We live in the age of science and the
conviction we have concerning God, or anything else
in fact, must be held in the light of all that science
has to say.

But this is not all. While acknowledging the service
science has rendered discrimination is necessary to
separate justifiable conclusions from questionable
statements which are not assured and which are repudiated by many scientists themselves. What are
we to do with this claim that we must lay aside the
belief in God as unscientific? One method has been to
counter the claim of these disbelievers by confronting
them with certain "proofs" of the existence of God
which cannot be controverted. If this could be done,
that is, if the so-called proofs were real proofs, it
would be a most effective method of dealing with the
problem. For when we use the word "proof" in the
strict sense it means something very definite and con-

vincing. A proof is something which cannot be gainsaid; it is final and authoritative. To deny its validity
is to render oneself liable to the charge of stubborn
ignorance or cause others to question one's mental
sanity. If one makes the claim that for him two
times two make five, he cannot be taken seriously.
He must believe that two times two make four, or
cease to do business with men and women in our
world. Now, when it is declared that we can prove
the existence of God what we mean is that a man
confronted with these proofs must acknowledge that
there is a God or be relegated to the same class with
those for whom two times two make five. And yet
when it is possible to find men who do not believe in
God and who are as honest as we are and are well
balanced mentally, we find ourselves led to ask
whether these proofs are what they claim to be. It is
necessary, then, for us to make an examination to
determine what may be expected of them.

Four of these arguments or proofs have had a long
history and come to us carrying the prestige of centuries of use. The first is the Cosmological, or the
argument from the existence of the universe in which
we live. The very fact of its existence implies a cause
or a creator. How can we account for it in any other
way? If anything takes place, it did not just happen;
there must be something which made it happen. Suppose we grant this, what have we achieved? Strictly
just this, that there is a cause adequate to produce
the result which is apparent to us, but that does not
mean that we may assert any significant thing about
that cause. All we are justified in saying is that
something caused this thing to take place. What is
this "something," this cause? If we say that it can

be nothing less than a personal God who willed to
create the universe, it may be true, as many of us
believe, but what right have we to do so on the
basis of the facts before us? Are we not reading into
our conclusion more than the facts justify? There
may be a personal Creator, but it is going beyond the
evidence with which we started to make such a declaration. There is nothing to compel us to come to
that conclusion.

Look at the Teleological argument, that from design. Everywhere around us there are evidences of
adaptation to ends. Things are as they are because
they were designed to fit into the scheme of things
and perform their part. Everywhere we see design—
must there not have been a Designer? That is the
argument. It was put far more crudely in the eighteenth century, before the doctrine of evolution spoiled
the nicety of the adaptations which were claimed for a
Designer who at the very beginning constructed each
organ to perform its appropriate function. Since the
evolutionary hypothesis has been so widely accepted
the argument has changed form. Instead of minute
adaptations which could be pointed to as the work of
an original Designer a more general adaptation has
to be asserted. The whole universe was so planned
that as it developed adaptations would take place as
they became necessary in nature and in human life.
But in either case the doubt rises in one's mind again
whether more is not read into the conclusion than the
premises justify. There are adaptations innumerable;
the very universe itself is what may be called a mutual universe, working together part with part as a
reciprocating unity. Does this, however, make it
altogether inevitable that we should conclude that a

personal Being is responsible for it? It may seem to be reasonable to one who already believes in a personal God, but that is a very different matter from claiming that we have a proof which a sane man can only disregard with peril. Design surely implies that there is something which makes it possible for adaptation to take place, but does it necessarily demand belief in a personal Designer who is responsible for it all? Hardly, when one considers the immense distance between the seemingly automatic adaptations in nature and the idea of the personal God of the Christian religion.

The third of the arguments is the Ontological. It has been put in a number of ways. Briefly stated it is this, that the presence in the mind of man of the conception of God is proof that such a God exists as an objective reality. As a formal argument it is a failure, and so cannot be used as a proof of the being of God. But this does not mean that the argument is of no use. It is helpful, as the two arguments previously presented are helpful, in giving a certain confidence to those who in other ways have arrived at the conclusion that there is a God. When one is so convinced it is quite natural that the presence of the God-idea in his mind will be accounted for by the presence of such a Being in the universe. But the point which is most salutary for everyone to see with great clearness is that all these arguments fail to compel belief in God among those who are not otherwise convinced. They may be helpful but they are not convincing; they point one to a most restful and satisfying conclusion, but they do not infallibly demonstrate the truth toward which they seem to move.

There is still another argument which has had a

long and honorable history, the Anthropological, the argument from the moral nature of man. And, although we must say the same of this argument as of the others so far as proof is concerned, we can readily use it as the basis on which we may start out on the positive side to answer the question with which this chapter started, How may I know there is a God?

The great question which every man faces as he looks out inquiringly into the limitless universe is how to account for it. Where can he find a sufficient ground for all the facts?—and insistence must be placed on taking account of *all* the facts. Yes, there are nature, the Milky Way, and the multiplication table—on what ground can they be explained? Power, wisdom, symmetry, and order are suggested—surely the ground of it all must be as much as is found in the product. But we cannot stop there, for life, personality, fellowship, morality, and conscience, the inalienable presence of religion in the world, are all as really parts of the universe as the more impersonal factors. The ground of the universe must be a sufficient explanation of these phenomena as of others. This is where the strength of the Anthropological argument lies—the moral nature of man must be taken into account.

When we sit down and carefully think it all over, the nature of the question which presents itself is this: Which is more likely, that the universe is to be explained by what is purely material and mechanical, or that another factor, that of living personality, must be introduced? Even if we might explain the cold, uninhabited moon as the result of impersonal energy, can we feel that it is a satisfactory explanation of Abraham Lincoln or one's mother? And we must remember that these personalities are as much a part of what demands explanation as an iceberg. And we must settle it for ourselves on the basis of what seems the more reasonable way of looking at it. The conclusion which I reach expresses the movement of my mind when it is brought into the presence of the facts.

This is not satisfactory to many. They say they desire to *know*, and that knowing must be something far more objectively verifiable than by a mere reference to one's personal reaction. But is such knowing possible in these matters? The conclusion already hinted at is that it is not; that if men are looking for such proofs of the existence of God that they can feel sure in the same way of that fact as they are of a sum in addition, they are doomed to disappointment. The Roman Catholic Church holds the contrary. To put it in the language of the Vatican Council of 1870, "If anyone shall say that the one and true God cannot be certainly known by the light of natural reason, let him be anathema." There are many outside the Roman Catholic Church who occupy a similar position. To them the whole theistic position would be seriously endangered unless the existence of God could be uncontrovertibly demonstrated. We have already tried to show that when this is attempted the results are disappointing. The arguments to prove the existence of God are helpful, but do not place the result securely beyond the reach of very annoying and disconcerting questions.

Is there no assurance besides that which comes out of one's inner consciousness? Undoubtedly, all of us are immeasurably helped by the testimony of others, men and women who in past ages as well as to-day have lived their lives in the quiet yet deep assurance that God is and that he hears and answers their prayers. This is one of the places where the Bible is most helpful. It does not try to prove the existence of God. It takes it for granted and then brings us into the company of great believers in God, so that we catch their assurance. But even when the full testimony of all these has been registered, is there not still a question remaining unanswered?

What does "knowing" mean when it is used of such high and important matters? If a thing cannot be demonstrated, how can we *know* it? If it is not susceptible of proof, what right have we to rest on the assertion that it is knowledge at all? Why not call it by another name and admit we are out of the realm of things that can be known? This is a fair question. I suppose the reason why we are not willing to do this is because we do not care to exclude from the circle of things known that which is most worth knowing, and also because we cannot get rid of the thought that this kind of knowing may be the noblest and most uplifting of which we are capable, because it makes demands of us which are not made in other kinds of knowing. To accept the multiplication table as true is easy; it would be more difficult to say it is not true than that it is, and when we accept it nothing significant happens within which affects character and life. This is stated almost to the point of exaggeration, for every assertion of truth makes us more truth-loving and teaches us to call things by their right names; but when all that is said, it is still apparent that there is a difference between asserting an axiomatic or demonstrable fact and asserting as fact what is not so nearly self-evident.

Knowing, then—to put it briefly, in the sense we have

now in mind—is to be so assured of a fact or a conclusion
that we are willing to put it to the test and act upon it.
In this kind of knowing we are active, not passive.
We rise to the thought and grapple with it, and can
never be the same again. We are theists because on
any other basis the world would be inexplicable or, at
least, more nearly chaotic than it is when we believe in
a Creator-God. Yet facts can be produced by the hundred to make such a conclusion difficult. Can there
be a God when Yokohama and Tokyo are suddenly
destroyed on a beautiful summer day? To believe in
God in the face of such a catastrophe can never be
achieved by going to a bookcase and reading a statement of the Teleological Argument from a musty
volume and pretending to be satisfied. Here is real
first-hand evidence; what are we going to do with it?
Without attempting here to deal with the problem of
the presence of suffering and evil in the universe, the
single statement may be made that we believe in God
because, even in face of an awful calamity, it is more
reasonable to do so than to deny it. But what makes
us come to that conclusion? Here is the key to the
whole question: We do so because it fits in better
with all we know and feel about what is and ought to
be than any other conclusion. It is a venture on the
basis of what we know to be truest and noblest within
ourselves. There must be a God, and he must be like
that, at least like that, or the universe is chaos. We
step out, test it—and what happens? We find that
the best in us responds and expands and that all life
takes on new meaning. The verification is that of life
and experience and not that of logic and proofs arrived at in the course of an argument. We take a
risk and we do not fail, that is, at the place where

failure or success really makes a difference, at the point of character. There is, then, that supreme element of faith, trusting ourselves and trusting the God who speaks in and through our truest selves when they are at their best.

How, to sum up what has been said, may I know there is a God? By acting as though there were a God, such a God as is demanded by the best in myself and in all those whom I respect, and seeing what happens. Then the assurance grows in one that there is a God and he will come to say "I know" in a deeper sense than he had ever dreamed of before.

CHAPTER II

WHAT KIND OF GOD DO WE HAVE?

CHRISTIANITY has but one God. It is distinguished from other religions by the nature and attributes of the God which it worships. Let us, however, at first look at the significance of the doctrine that there is but one God.

Monotheism has had a most interesting history. Even now the ideas concerning the development of the monotheistic idea are being changed. If one turns to the writings of such a scholar as J. G. Frazer he will find the claim made that man was animistic in his earliest period and then developed into a stage when the indefinite godlings of the animistic stage developed into the great and distinct gods of polytheism. The names of many of these gods are well known, both in ancient times and to-day. Marduk, Zeus, Mars, Amida, Vishnu come to mind at once. Then, according to Frazer and others, we began to find monotheistic ideas permeating the minds of men until in the higher religions, such as Judaism, Mohammedanism, and Christianity, there has developed the doctrine of one God and one God only. In recent years, however, a very interesting fact has come to light, namely, that even among primitive peoples there exists the idea of an "All-Father." This does not carry with it the exclusion of all other gods, but it does convey the idea that at least some of these people were aware of another factor in addition to

the many gods of their animism and that they had
begun even in their undeveloped condition to reach out
after what later developed into real monotheism.   They
did not reach it but it was a real movement in that
direction.   This discovery of high gods was disconcerting, because, according to Frazer and other strict
evolutionists, men in the animistic stage of development could not think monotheistically.   We know
better now.   Professor Radin, in his recent volume,
Monotheism Among Primitive Peoples, expresses the
opinion that among the deeper spirits even in animistic religion there came a time when they began to
think thoughts which were almost monotheistic if not
completely so.   It would seem to indicate, at any
rate, that man did not have to develop into the possibility of such thoughts but was ready for them if
they were clearly suggested to him at any time in his
history.

In discussing the development of the Christian conception of God our chief concern is with the growth of
the idea of God in the Old and New Testaments.   The
significant truth should be appreciated that during
the longer period of the history of the Hebrew race
as it is recounted in the Old Testament the Israelites
were henotheists and not monotheists.   They believed that there was but one God for them and for
their land, but that other peoples must have their
own separate gods, because they were a different
people and lived outside the land which was pe-
culiarly the possession of the God of Israel.   This
continued down to the time of the writing prophets,
to the time of Amos and Hosea and Isaiah.

One of the earliest approaches to the monotheistic
idea is to be found in the first two chapters of the

book of Amos. It is exceedingly important to understand the approach to the doctrine which is found there. It is in no sense an intellectual or philosophical statement; it is distinctively moral. Amos became convinced that the moral law applied to all peoples and that the sameness of the moral law could only be explained by sameness of origin. God was the God of all peoples because all had done wrong and all were to be punished in the same moral world in which they all lived. This is quite distinctive of the Old Testament viewpoint and is very unlike the approach to the monotheistic position which was reached by the Greeks, particularly Plato and Aristotle. For them God was one because their intellect demanded it. It was incongruous for them to think of a universe which was becoming more and more unified in their minds with more than one single God, who was its ground and explanation. To the Hebrews, however, God became the one God of the universe because they lived in a moral world over which one holy God, the only one, could be thought of as ruling. It is the peculiar combination of oneness and holiness which characterizes the conception of God in the Old Testament and which was the great gift of the Old Testament to the New. God was not only one; he was just as essentially holy. To a Jew of the later Old Testament period it would be no more foolish to speak of many gods than to speak of one God for whom sin was not necessarily an abhorrence. To be God for them was to be one who hated sin and loved righteousness. Cleavage between good and evil seemed to them to go back into the very nature of God himself. The result of it all was that we have the possibility of the revelation of God in Jesus Christ in the New Testament, for only on such a foundation could a religion like Christianity be built.

Christianity, then, has appropriated the Old Testament conception of God. The God revealed by Jesus Christ was the one God of the universe who was essentially holy. Jesus, it is true, emphasized certain features which needed emphasis, but the foundation upon which he built was the foundation laid by the Old Testament prophets. No clearer statement of monotheism can be found than those wonderful statements in the latter part of the book of Isaiah, where the utter foolishness of believing in the existence of other gods is stated as clearly as anywhere in all literature.

Jesus did add, however, to our conception of God by showing even more clearly what God was like. He was the one God to be sure and he was holy, but Jesus made us see that he was also our Father. This does not mean that God had never been pictured as a Father before. What it does mean is that Jesus raised the conception of God as Father into such prominence that it resulted in an actual change of name. The real name for our God is not Jehovah, as it was in the Old Testament, but the name with which Jesus made us familiar, "Our Father." The peculiar quality in this idea of fatherhood which Jesus proclaimed was love. God to Jesus was love, and the best commentary we have on the love of God is the life and teaching of Jesus himself. God is what we see expressed in Jesus Christ, in terms we can understand. So true is this that one of the most profound and significant statements to be made about God is to say that he is like Jesus Christ—our God is a Christlike God. We need to realize clearly the wonder of this conception. Jesus did not in any sense minimize the awful holiness of God as he is depicted in the Old Testament, but he added to that moral concern a peculiar emphasis on love, a love which goes to the point of suffering and sacrifice in order that men may be brought back into the family of God whose unity had been broken by wrongdoing.

This God of the Old Testament and the God whom Jesus revealed more clearly is a personal God. It seems almost unnecessary to make mention of this feature because when we speak of God in terms of Jesus we can only think of him as personal. But it is necessary for us to go a step further and ask what we mean when we speak of God as personal. Does it mean that he is personal only in the sense in which we are? Surely this could not be true, for we are finite, and God evidently must be infinite. We are weak and God is just the opposite. We are sinful and God is absolutely pure. Not only is this true, but in all those features which go to make up our personality there seems to be the finger mark of imperfection upon them. What, then, do we mean when we say that God is personal? It may best be stated in this form: that God is personal in the sense that we may enter into relations with him as we do with our fellow human beings. We have personal relations with each other. We may have relationship with God as we do with our fellows here below. Coming to it from this standpoint we do not tie ourselves up to any narrow or unworthy conception of God, but it does make possible the thought that God with all his majesty is still enough like ourselves to be able to hold communion with us. Is not this at least one of the meanings which we express when we say that God made man in his own image? We were made in the image of God that we might hold fellowship with him.

This brings us to the important question as to the possibility of using human analogies in describing God. Let us realize that one of the greatest dangers which men have encountered is that of describing God in anthropomorphic terms, which is just to say that we describe God on the basis of human analogies. The difficulty in the past has been that God has been declared to be so much like man that many of the weaknesses of humanity have been carried up into the divine life itself. In the non-Christian religions gods are unworthy in many cases even of the respect of humanity. The gods of Mount Olympus became the laughing stock of the finer spirits of later Greek history. Plato definitely turned against them and said that the presentation of such characters would lower the moral level of those to whom such instruction was given. Here anthropomorphism is a dangerous feature of religious life. The gods were pictured very much like men, and like men in their weaknesses rather than in their strength.

We cannot get away, however, from the anthropomorphic idea by these criticisms. Suppose we do not use human analogies, how can we describe God? The fact is we cannot describe him at all. He would be utterly opaque and unknowable to human beings. This is exactly the conclusion reached by orthodox Mohammedanism, which when it says that God is merciful hastens to inform the reader that God is not merciful in any sense in which man is merciful. He is just "merciful," and we must accept it at that without attempting to attach any definite meaning to the phrase. Fortunately, we are not driven into such

a difficult position in Christianity. What we say is
that God is like man in certain respects, but not in
all. He is omnipotent, to be sure, but men have
power, too, and on the basis of power as we see it displayed among men we say that God has power, only
that he has it to a degree beyond the possibilities of
man. Our ability to do things points in the right
direction, although we can never reach the complete
idea of the meaning of God's omnipotence. We say
that God is omniscient, and the only meaning we can
attach to that term is on the basis that we also have
some knowledge and that God's knowledge is at least
something like that. God's knowledge includes everything in its survey as contrasted with the meagerness
of our own outlook. But we do know some things
sufficiently for the purpose of analogy. Were it not
for this God would be utterly unknowable. When we
are told, however, that we were created in God's
own image, we are fully justified in using human
analogies in our attempt to understand something of
the nature of God. When, finally, he was revealed in
Jesus Christ as Father, our ideas were enlarged as we
were led to think of God in terms of human fatherhood, not completely interpreted by what we see of
fatherhood among ourselves but more fully by the
way in which Jesus acted as he came in contact with
men and women.

We have just spoken of two of the great attributes
of God, omnipotence and omniscience. Are we to
look upon these attributes as absolute? That is, are
we to say when we declare God omnipotent that he
can do whatever he wills? There is no doubt that
every Christian would say that God can do whatever
he wills without limit if that limitation is thought of

as something outside himself. It would be abhorrent
to us to think that God was hindered from the ac-
complishment of his purposes by a great cosmic force
which he himself could not control.

The contrast between the Christian and Mohammedan viewpoints is helpful. The Mohammedan would
say that God must be conceived as omnipotent in the
absolute sense; that is, God can do whatever he wills
and nothing can stand in the way of that will. This
sounds like a Christian idea, but one step more reveals
that it is not. The Mohammedan would put the will
of God as the primary factor in determining what
God is and can do. The Christian attitude is somewhat different. The final factor in the being of God
is not his will but his nature. The very structure of
the being of God itself determines what the will shall
do. Back of the will of God is his eternal nature
which is holy and loving. The will of God is not
limited by any force or power outside himself, but is
limited by his nature which determines all that he
does. God cannot do evil, because his nature is good.
God cannot be unloving, because his nature is love.
Our God is not a capricious God, as is the Mohammedan Allah, who may will to do one thing to-day and
its opposite to-morrow. Our God is a God the law of
whose nature is unchanging. He is the God of holiness and the God of love and we may count upon that
righteousness and that love to the utmost.

There is, however, another feature in God's relationship to his creation which must be carefully considered. Is God limited at the point of his relationship with the men he has created? Such extreme
determinists as Mohammedans go to the extreme of
fatalism and hold that God is not limited in any way

even in his relationship to his creatures. They hold that men do not have any kind of essential freedom, but that everything is so determined that what the will of God foreordains must come to pass whatever men may think or do about it. Many Christians, while not holding such an extreme view, have approximated it. But it does not represent the facts. God in creation, particularly in the creation of man, voluntarily limited himself. He did so in order that the fundamental desire of his heart might be expressed, the desire for the love and fellowship of human beings who might freely accept him. There could, however, be no freedom in this acceptance unless God's power were limited so that he might not coerce human beings to accept him. Only on this basis is it possible to conceive of the building up of a race of men and women who are worthy of fellowship with a moral God. The fellowship must be on the basis of righteousness, and it could not be on that basis unless on the ground of real freedom, a freedom which gives significance to all of our thoughts and deeds. God, then, is a God who in the wonder of his purpose was willing to be limited in order that ultimately there might be built up a race of those who could experience through the eternities that fellowship with him which is the climax of all personal relationships in the universe.

The Christian doctrine of God has always insisted upon a combination of two relations which have been held separately in many places and times in the history of religion. There are those, particularly in India, who believe that God is to be identified with his universe. They are pantheists, who hold that there is no God beyond the universe which reveals him, that all

that is is God and God is all there is. There are two
very dangerous tendencies at work in this theory
which have been amply demonstrated wherever pantheism has been able to work itself out through long
periods. Human personality suffers, because wherever
pantheism is presented there is the tendency to deny
the rights of distinct personality. Everything ultimately sinks back into God, the All, and whenever
this process has done its complete work among men
the dulling of personality always results. In destroying the idea of personality in God man's worth as an
individual begins to diminish. The other danger has
been that ethical distinctions tend to be lost. If God
is the Absolute and incorporates within himself everything that is, evil is a part of God as much as righteousness. If that be true the distinction between
righteousness and evil is only a seeming or a temporary distinction. Ultimately when we see things as
they are the line of demarcation will be blotted out
and we shall see that there is no difference between
right and wrong. The result of this among men is
always that insistence upon a righteous life becomes
secondary to other considerations not so fundamental
in human nature. Yet the Athenians were told by
Paul that we live and move and have our being in
God. This looks in the direction of the theory we
have just been discussing but with a significant difference. In pure pantheism the ideal is so complete
an identification with God that the identity of the
individual human being is completely submerged and
lost. In Christianity, on the other hand, there is
pictured a union of God and man so close that there
is a common purpose. What God wills, man wills;
what God loves, man loves. But through it all the

man retains his individual identity. He is not merged in God; he lives with God. The life he lives is in such intimate fellowship that Paul could say of it that it was no longer he that lived, but Christ lived in him, yet without the suggestion that Paul himself ceased to be. He was still Paul, but Paul dominated by God and drawing his life from God.

The other tendency is that of separating God so far from his world that men cannot come into close relations with him. This doctrine was announced with great confidence by certain writers in England who were called Deists in the eighteenth century. They believed in God, in one God who was righteous, but a God who when he had created the world, wound it up, as it were, and left it almost to its own devices. Not that the world was self-sustaining, but that so far as any intimate connection between man and God was concerned there was no hope that any human being could have such a relationship. God was altogether transcendent, he was "high and lifted up" above man, with no possibility of prayer and of such answers as would show man that God heard and was willing to do things which otherwise he would not do for his needy children. There can be no doubt that God must be presented as by Isaiah when he sees him in majesty on his throne. God is the Creator and Sustainer of the universe, but this is not the whole truth. For Christians he is also near at hand. It is in him we live and move and have our being. It is only by a combination of the immanence and the transcendence of God that we can formulate such a doctrine as will satisfy all the demands of human life. And this is what Christianity does. It is by no means an easy matter to hold the balance between these two tendencies. The history of religion in the world is an ample demonstration of that. But nevertheless it must be done. Christianity cannot continue to exist unless God is presented both as the one who is closer to us "than breathing and nearer than hands and feet," and at the same time as one who is outside ourselves, into whose being we are never to merge but with whom we are to have fellowship, a fellowship of the kind which is only possible between a great Father who is the lover of all and his children who have come to realize what that love means and who have deliberately chosen to enter in and share its wonder and its glory.

CHAPTER III

IS THE GOD WHO CREATED THE WORLD A GOOD GOD?

THE question which has been asked in this study can only arise for one who is a monotheist. Evil exists in the universe in which we live. This presents no difficulty for one who believes in more than one god, for there may be a division of responsibility, with one god the creator of good and others responsible for evil. But for the monotheist, who believes there is but one God, the Creator and Sustainer of the universe, there is a real problem. How can we make good our claim that God is good when we see so much evil and suffering in the universe?

The whole problem of evil in the universe presses at several points. We may glance at these points in order and then go back and consider them more in detail. The universe seems so heartless in the utter impartiality of its dealings with man. How can there be a good God when the good are treated just as the wicked in the world in which we live? Why should there be so much suffering in the realm of a good and kindly God? How can we justify the presence of sin in a universe planned, we are told, to exalt righteousness?

At the very beginning of the consideration of these questions it is necessary to state that, while help may be available, complete light is beyond the bounds of possibility. It may be well to quote from L. P. Jacks, in his helpful volume, *Religious Perplexities*. He says: "We can change the nature of our religious perplexities, change them from things that depress into things that exalt us, but we cannot banish them altogether. At the end of our labors, as at the beginning, we shall find ourselves perplexed, *but not unto despair*. These last words make the difference, and it is immense."[1] We may believe that there is reason in the universe to a certain extent, but our poor human knowledge and wisdom run out before we have gotten even within sight of our goal. God's ways are not our ways and can never be completely understood by us. The temptation is to drop the whole subject and let the matter rest, attempting to keep ourselves from facing the problem more frequently than is absolutely necessary. This, however, is an unworthy course. If we are to have peace in this world at all, it can only come after we have faced all the ugly facts in it. We are bound to use our reason as far as it will reach, and in doing so we shall find that real help will be forthcoming along the way. We shall discover, however, that there are difficulties unsolved, but fortunately for us, as Principal Jacks declares, we may be perplexed, "but not unto despair."

The first question to be faced is that with reference to the heartless, impartial universe in which we live. But suppose it were otherwise. Suppose whenever a bad man falls down he should hurt himself, and whenever a good man falls down he would not. What kind of universe would that be? It surely should be far more topsy-turvy than it is now. It would be undependable. No confidence could be placed in its opera-

---

[1] Reprinted by permission of George H. Doran Company, Publishers. Copyright 1923.

tions. In a world where good and evil are so inextricably mingled, as we find about us on every side, we would not get along at all if the operations of nature were determined by the moral character of the various individuals in it. It is far better to live in a universe where we may know that whether a man is good or bad the laws of gravitation will always hold. It may be a heartless universe, but, after all, impartiality is something we can understand and take account of. We can accommodate our lives to such a universe far better than to one where good is rewarded in the very processes of nature itself. No, God makes his sun to shine on the evil and on the good. Surely, it is not difficult to justify the ways of God with man so far as his creation and its uniform laws are concerned.

Where the problem pinches is when affliction comes to this or that person. We may be able to arrive at some general theory which satisfied as a theory, and fail completely to see in particular cases what meaning there can be in some so-called "Providence." On the whole the system is an expression of God's wisdom, but in particular cases we fail to fathom the meaning of some stroke of nature. Why should a strong man, the support of his wife, be taken away and she, a poor invalid not able to care for herself, be left? A hundred illustrations leap to one's mind when he begins to think of these unaccountable occurrences. God may have good reason why these things happen, but with all the accumulated wisdom of the ages we are just as far from a solution of the problem in particular cases as men were in the beginning. It becomes an act of faith when we are able to say that while we cannot understand what has happened, we still believe that it was permitted by a good God and that ultimately we too will be able to enter into its meaning.

The whole question becomes even more difficult when afflictions take the form of suffering and pain. Again, however, we must realize that suffering and pain are a part of the natural order of the universe and are not caused, except in specific cases, by sin. God is responsible for them and they run back to a time far beyond the days when man first did wrong. Our knowledge of animals, their history and their anatomy, clearly shows that suffering and death were present long before sin entered into the world and man did wrong and thus brought added suffering to himself and to his fellows. Death has assumed a different form among men because of wrongdoing, but death itself is not the punishment of sin. It is well known among students of science that death is a biological necessity, if there is to be any advance at all or any racial development. It can only be on the basis of the passing away of former generations that those who are younger can take advantage of new light and step out into a world which is a real improvement on that which has gone before.

Much discussion has been aroused by the question as to whether animals suffer as much as we think they do. The consensus of opinion seems to be that while animals do really suffer, it is not as severe as it is with men and women. We suffer in anticipation because we are human beings. Animals have comparatively little of this imaginative power, which is so large a part of our suffering. But even when we have minimized the suffering as far as science will allow, there is still an enormous amount of pain staring all living creatures in the face. When we begin to consider the suffering caused by cancer and other illnesses, there is no wonder that once in a while a man here or a woman there has serious doubts as to the goodness of a God who would permit such suffering as they see in the pain-racked bodies of their friends and dear ones.

With all this, however, it is possible to see a meaning in pain. It has a real function to perform. It is a warning of danger and is educative in the highest sense. It is a most difficult discipline, to be sure, but without it we would scarcely be worth caring for. Without pain—and here we may enlarge the term to cover not only the pain of the body but mental pain and spiritual torment—there would be no stimulus to work, to achieve, and to make advance. In the words of Professor George Galloway, "A painless body and a perfectly tractable environment would have meant no progress."[1] One can almost become eloquent in attempting to show the place occupied by pain and discomfort in human life, yet here again, while it is quite possible to arrive at a theory which satisfies more or less, when we come to particular cases it is impossible to see reason in what is taking place. Why should this person suffer as he does, especially when it may be a perfectly innocent man or a dear little child?

It is when we come into the realm of moral evil that we approach the deepest and the most harassing problem of all. However it may be explained, sin exists in the universe. Why should it be there? Does God will it as a necessity? Does he permit it, either as inevitable or as a means to some end? Does it exist as an outlaw in God's universe? If so, must we

[1] Used by permission of Charles Scribner's Sons.

not say that God is not in complete control of the very universe which he created? Here are the alternatives. There seem to be no others, and ultimately it will be necessary for us to make a choice in order to have some ground on which to rest.

But there are those who would say with the philosopher Hegel that we should not make so much of sin. After all it is "good in the making." It must be looked upon simply as a negative and inevitable counterpart to the positive good around us. There are those who would even go so far as to say that "the way to virtue lies through sin." The attitude of Christian Science is virtually in agreement with the monistic philosophy of Hegel. "Sin, like other kinds of evil, is only a seeming evil, a disease of mortal mind." As soon as we are able to look on it differently it disappears as a real entity in the universe. The mistake is in our interpretation; change that and all difficulty disappears.

But for the vast majority of men and women in the world it is impossible to accept any such explanation. Sin is too real and ugly for that. Their own conscience condemns them and remorse fills their hearts. They are conscious that there is something about sin which ought not to be and that it might be prevented. They may not know exactly how, but nevertheless they rebel at the thought of its presence in the world and will not believe that it can make any contribution to the uplift of man. They are perfectly willing to agree that physical pain may be educative; they are not willing to agree that any good thing can come out of sin.

Then if sin is a positive and destructive thing, who is responsible for it? If the universe and everything in it are determined by the divine decrees or by the laws according to which it operates, God must be solely responsible for sin. If we do what is determined by forces over which we have no control, then we are no longer responsible. But again the voice of conscience is heard and the sense of guilt becomes almost intolerable. Our very natures cry out that we have a certain power of choice, that we are free and therefore responsible. But when we make man responsible for sin because of his freedom, we have by no means said the final word. We admit that sin is actually to be found in the universe which God has created. So inevitably God has some connection with it, for he might have made the universe on a different plan according to which sin might not even have been a possibility. We cannot completely absolve God even by declaring that man is free and that sin came into being because of that freedom.

The problem is so pressing and so distressing, however, that the attempt has been made to meet it by declaring that God is only good and that we cannot think of him as being in any way responsible for evil in the world. Some would say that sin is against his will and that if he had had his way it would never have appeared in the universe at all. They hold that it is altogether intolerable to believe that God even permitted it for any purpose whatsoever in the universe which he has created. Mr. H. G. Wells and others believe that the God we worship, or ought to worship, is only partly responsible for conditions in the world, that he is a "Finite God" who does not know exactly how things are coming out, but asks our cooperation that we may together with him bring in a new day in which sin shall be banished. While this theory has been grasped at by some, even among Christian leaders, as a welcome relief from a thorny conclusion, it would seem to one who has any conception of the real difficulty that it is only pushing the problem one step further back. If the God we know is not responsible for the evil in the universe, who is? Is there some inscrutable power back of the God we know? If so, our God is a puny God contrasted with that power, and we automatically become just as much interested in finding out what the nature of that responsible power is as we have ever been to find out about God. If that "power" is not good, there is no assurance that goodness is at the heart of the universe. There is not even the assurance that things will come out right in the end, for a finite God is finite, no matter how much we might clothe him with glory and honor. It would seem far better to live in a universe whose God is the Creator and Controller of everything, even though we are unable to give a complete explanation of the presence of sin in that universe, than it would be to believe in a God who is altogether good, but whose goodness is not coupled with power and omnipotence and back of whom is some dark unknown Something which is responsible for evil and which is greater than God himself. There is little to be hoped for by this attempt to find release from our difficulties. It really plunges us more deeply into the shadows than ever.

But we have still our problem to meet. Here is a world which God created, and sin is in it. How can we justify ourselves in speaking of God as good? We need to be very careful to make an important distinction, that God made a universe with the possibility of evil in it, and not a universe in which evil existed as it came out of his hands or a universe in which evil was inevitable. The real question is to determine, if possible, why God should construct a universe in which the possibility of sin was present. The only answer to be given is that if evil were not possible good would not be possible either. Goodness is not a passive thing. It is the free choice of what is godlike on the part of the men whom God has made, and there could be no goodness unless the choice were between actual possibilities, a possibility of evil and a possibility of good. God was confronted with the problem of making a world of automatons or of making a world of human beings. As soon as he had decided, if we may speak with reverence, to make a race of human beings he had settled the question by that decision that there must be the possibility of evil in it. For whenever human freedom, which makes human beings what they are, exists there is the open choice lying before each man and woman to decide for godlikeness or to decide against it.

We may even push the question further back and ask, Why was it necessary to make such a race? Again we can only answer partially, but it does seem to be clear that God desired humanity for fellowship with himself, and fellowship with a God whose very being is righteousness could only be achieved on the plane of the qualities which are inherent in the nature of God himself. God would not be God at all if he were not holy and loving and righteous. To have fellowship with such a God real righteousness is demanded, and this can only come by choice on the part of the men and women who were thus made in order that they might have fellowship with God himself. Professor James Ward declares, in substance, that the possibility of moral evil is implied in any moral order that is evolved at all.

It becomes apparent that God took a great risk in creating man. He could have created a race without the possibility of moral evil and there would have been no risk, but he chose the other course. The result was that evil came and is with us now, but we must be careful to make the distinction already spoken of that moral evil is not inevitable to ourselves. It is avoidable. What is necessary to maintain of the universe is the possibility of evil, and it is this possibility that makes character possible. Character is achieved only through conflict and resistance, only because men have the power of choice. This is the kind of universe God planned and brought into existence. We can see reason in it, but still many things in the nature of the case remain obscure and difficult.

CHAPTER IV

HOW WAS THE WORLD CREATED?

THE idea of creation is necessary in any Christian statement of the origin of the world. Whatever may be the theory we adopt concerning the manner in which it took place and the length of time consumed in the process, it is a process of creation which is always in mind.

We use the term with considerable ease, but scarcely realize how difficult the conception of creation is. We ourselves fashion many things from pre-existing material. We make tables and chairs and build houses and trolley cars and what-not, but that is not what is meant by creation. If we should attribute any such fashioning of the universe to God, we might be led into the futilities of an "infinite regress." If at each time creation is mentioned we should only assert that it was but a rearrangement of something which already existed, instead of settling the question we would be merely pushing the difficulty a step further back. What we mean when we say that God created the world is that he did something original, that something came into existence which did not exist before in any form.

But before dealing with the meaning of such a conception we must realize that the statement made in the first chapter of Genesis is not at all clear. Scholars are of the opinion that the account in Genesis does not make any statement about the absolute and original creation of the world, but that God made the ordered universe in which we live out of what was "waste and void." There is evidence that there was something already in existence, a kind of chaos, which was fashioned into a cosmos by the action of God upon it. It must be made clear that our desire to think of an absolute beginning was not shared by people living in the distant past. They were not so much interested in an original creation as in being able to account for the fact that the universe is what it actually appears to be. This viewpoint, however, does not satisfy us to-day at all. We want to feel that God not only fashioned the existing universe out of a chaos with which he had to work, but that he was Creator in the sense that nothing exists for which God is not completely responsible. Many have sought to state the fact by declaring that God created the world "out of nothing." Whatever happened, this phrase does not enlighten us. It is really a blanket for our ignorance. "Nothing" is just what it says; it is nothing, and so we do not learn how God created the universe when we say that he created the universe out of nothing.

We have no human analogies to help us to understand the meaning of God's creative act. The nearest we can come to it is what we know of the creative work of some genius among men. Beethoven may be spoken of as a creator, for while he used many ideas which came to him from others, after all there is something about the product of his genius which must be spoken of as original and which expresses his mind and purpose in a unique way. And yet even this is not a complete analogy of what we know as "creation" when thought of as God's act. But anything which will help us to understand is to be welcomed. Any creative genius is so wonderful and stands out so high above those around him that we are lifted to a higher plane by attempting to account for what such a genius accomplishes. What, then, do we mean when we say that God created the world? Probably it may be put in this way as well as in any other: that the world is not self-existent or independent. It could neither come into existence nor continue to exist at all without God. What we mean to assert is that there is an absolute dependence on God as the originator of everything that is. He is its only explanation. He only is the reason for its existence. It is not possible to overemphasize this fact. God created, brought something into being, holds it in existence to-day, and does it so effectively that nothing can be thought of as existent unless at the same time we think of its dependence upon the will of God both in original creation and in its continued existence.

So far there is comparatively little difficulty. We have merely been trying to clarify what all Christians believe. When we come, however, to ask about the time element and the method which the universe itself discloses concerning God's relation to it, we run into difficulty. What about the theory of evolution? The question we face is, Do we not prove the Bible untrue and that God is unnecessary and that man loses his dignity when we declare that evolution is the method by which things came into existence? Here is where the problem presses, and it is wise to deal with each of the features mentioned separately and very carefully.

The Bible declares in the first chapter of Genesis that the world was created in six days, and that on the seventh day God rested from his labor. I do not think it is necessary here to enter into the question as to the relation of this account to that in the second chapter of Genesis. If anyone will read the first chapter (and the first three verses of the second chapter) and then the second chapter of Genesis, he will find that there is some difficulty in telling exactly what the biblical account of creation is. There are differences which can scarcely be harmonized concerning the time and the order of the separate creative acts. Taking the statement as we find it in the first chapter of the Bible, I believe there is no legitimate method of proving that the "days" which are mentioned are anything else than twenty-four-hour days. The best proof of this position is the fourth commandment, in which we are told that men should keep the seventh day, because on that day God rested after his labor during the six previous days. The analogy is very clear. We are to rest through the same period that God rested, namely, the seventh day. It is only those who have felt the pressure of the revelations of science who have tried to extend the word "day" to make it include long periods of time.

The theory of evolution makes it clear that the universe was a long period coming into its present state, and that the process is still going on. There certainly seems to be a head-on collision at this point. What are we to do about it? May I say very frankly that I believe we are going to do about it just what we have done with other points of difficulty in the past. When Copernicus and Galileo made their discoveries, we accepted them, very hesitatingly it is true, but we accepted them, even though they ran contrary to the viewpoint of the Bible that the earth is flat and is the center of our solar system, in fact, of the entire universe. No one had the slightest idea before that time that the earth was a round ball swinging in space, a very small body in an unthinkably immense expanse in which there were many other worlds larger than our earth. If one goes back and reads the story of the persecution and the condemnation of those who were willing to assert what everyone believes to-day, it might give us pause when we condemn what the evolutionists declare is the reasonable view of the method of the creation of the universe. We are not asked to-day to do anything essentially different from what our fathers did a few hundred years ago.

Concerning Copernicus it was said, "This fool wishes to reverse the entire science of astronomy." This charge was true, and the astounding fact is that he did it. John Calvin said of his work, "Who will venture to place the authority of Copernicus above that of the Holy Ghost?" Yet we all accept the theories of Copernicus to-day! John Owen declared that this teaching was a "A delusive and arbitrary hypothesis, contrary to Scripture." John Wesley spoke of it as something which "tends to infidelity." We are not being asked to-day to accept a conclusion more difficult or strange than that of the universe as described by the prophets of science of a former day who have also proved to be prophets of God.

No one believes to-day that the earth is at the center of the solar system, not to speak of its being at the center of the celestial universe, and yet wherever the matter is mentioned in the Bible, it is taken for granted that what we do not now believe is actually the fact. Anyone who will take the time to study the fears which men had when Columbus and other navigators started out across an unknown sea will realize that one of the difficulties was that men thought the earth was flat, and that they would come to a place where it ended, and if they went further they would fall over the brink. Where would they go? The answer may be given in the words of one who, upon being asked why it was that the sun became so red as it went down over the western horizon, answered that it was because "it looketh down on hell." It was a very small and limited universe in which men lived in that day. We do not agree with them, and it is impossible to do so. The facts have been too strong for us, and facts will have their way in the end.

This, however, does not help us constructively to know what to do about the Bible. Is there any clue to a satisfying conclusion? There seems to be one and only one which fulfills all the conditions necessary to such a solution. It is that the science of the Bible must be looked upon as the science of the time when its writers lived. The Bible is a book which came out of definite historical situations, and it speaks the language which would be understood by those for whom it was written. It must of necessity speak in the terms which were used and understood at that time with reference to nature and the universe as well as about everything else. Not one single modern discovery is predicted in the Bible. None of the accepted conclusions of scientific investigation could even be guessed at by reading the accounts of the natural world as found in the Scripture. We must remember that science is always changing and developing. If we study carefully, we shall see that even in the Bible the ethical standards were changing and that Jesus could rightly declare that certain things were said to them of olden time, but that we must correct it by taking a different attitude. Have we ever stopped to think that if science and the Bible should be in exact agreement to-day, it would be the first time that such an agreement had existed, and also the last? It is of the very nature of science—in fact, of the human mind itself when it is awake—to seek for more and more of the meaning of the universe, and the wonderful thing about the universe is that it is so marvelous that we have only been able to touch its fringes. There is much more to be learned than we know now, and no possibility exists of men being able to prevent others from continuing their study by telling them that their conclusions must always be in exact accord with the facts concerning the universe as given in the Bible.

We must learn to look upon our Scriptures not as a book of science but as a book of ethics and of religion. When we turn to the Bible for that which will tell us how we shall live with our neighbor and how we should live before God, when we go to the Bible to find out the meaning of our lives and the kind of God with whom we deal, the Bible remains to this day the one incomparable book in the world. It is just as up to date now as it was when it was written. We need to appreciate the fact that the Bible is the great "classic" of religion and morality. What do we mean when we say that any writing is a classic? Probably this at least, that human nature was seen so clearly by the writer that, having penetrated far down under the surface to its depths, he found out what was eternally true. Human nature does not change fundamentally, and therefore any time in history when a man like

Homer or Shakespeare is able to tell us the truth about human nature it is always true. There is something eternal about truth. In some such sense, though to a far greater extent, the Bible is the one book in the world which has plumbed human nature and has given us a revelation of God as he really is. Let us realize that since God remains the same and human nature is the same, whenever any book says something true of God and men, it is always true. The glory of the Bible is in the fact that it presents us with Jesus Christ. Having done that there is a finality about the book which can never be superseded. What we must do is to allow the Bible to speak out its message, which is a religious and ethical message and not a message concerning science, which must be changing from time to time to be true to itself and to its God-given task.

There is a second danger which has been mentioned, namely, that evolution makes God unnecessary. Is that true? It all depends upon what kind of evolution we have in our minds. There is an evolution which would make God unnecessary, the form of evolution which is purely materialistic or mechanistic. It is the evolution which says that, given matter and force, everything in the universe may be accounted for without God, without any personal element as essential to it. This kind of evolution would destroy any Christian faith. We need to be very clear and frank at this point. It is not because it is evolution that it is destructive, but because of the philosophy which lies back of it. It rests on the supposition that the ultimate reality lying back of the universe as we know it is not personal but material and mechanical. It is exceedingly interesting that this materialism can exist and has existed as an explanation of the universe without connection with the theory of evolution. Whenever God and personality are ruled out there is great danger, whether it be connected with the theory of evolution or not. The danger is not in the evolution, which is a scientific theory, but in a materialistic philosophy which has no necessary connection with the particular scientific theory to which it has attached itself.

One of the most significant facts in the world of science to-day is that there are many evolutionists who repudiate materialism as heartily as the confirmed literalist in biblical interpretation. To them God is altogether necessary. The God they believe in and worship is not an impersonal force but a personal God who is to them the God and Father of our Lord Jesus Christ. They can explain nothing in the universe without him. He is an absolute necessity in their thinking, as they try to account for the universe which they are investigating. They are believers in God and are frequently spoken of as theistic evolutionists. They believe that evolution was the method of creation, but it did not run itself. Evolution is to them the method by which the great God proceeded in his work of creating. To them it seems more wonderful for God to have been engaged through the ages in the process of bringing the world into being than it would be for him to speak just one word about six thousand years ago and to bring into existence all the wonder of the world in which we live. The records which are in the rocks are to them the touch of the finger of God, and reveal to them the method of God's creation which is past understanding and yet which gives evidence of a wisdom which seems the more wonderful as through the ages of the past God has been making our universe to be what it is. And it seems no less wonderful to them that God is not at work sustaining the universe as a static, undeveloped mass of material, but that his fingers are still deftly at work continuing the process in order that in the end even more beauty may be apparent in a universe which already fills them with admiration.

There is still another fear which is expressed by those who look with dread upon the coming of any theory which is not in literal accord with the account in the first chapter of Genesis. Will not man lose his dignity if an animal ancestry is asserted? It may not be out of place to mention in passing that no evolutionist to-day believes that man is descended from a monkey. The theory held by all biologists to-day is that the monkey sprang from the stem of the anthropoid apes which also at a later time was the stem from which men were developed. This, of course, is not in any sense to minimize the statement that man has an animal ancestry, that is, so far as his body and certain mental characteristics are concerned. Should we be fearful at this point we must remember that according to the second chapter of Genesis, which differs in this respect from the first chapter, man was fashioned out of pre-existing material. It was the "dust of the earth." The evolutionist agrees that man was made out of earthly material, but by a long process of development, and that before the earthly material was fit to be molded into the form of a man it was transformed many times over through lower forms into higher forms until at last there came a time when man could be given a soul, that which differentiates him from the animals with whom he is related in other ways. Mr. William Jennings Bryan and his friends do not see that man can be descended from lower forms through an animal ancestry and at the same time be created in God's image. Why man cannot be as much in God's image if he arose by a very long process from earthly material through animal forms as if he were made out of material dust by an immediate word of God is hard to understand.

The one great fact which is incontrovertible is that man's body gives evidence that it belongs to the animal creation and that it has had an animal ancestry. But while this cannot be gainsaid, it is not as significant as another which we must hasten to make, that he is the only animal who is more than animal. It was Aristotle who said that man was a "political animal." It remained for Christians to raise him to a higher dignity and speak of him as a spiritual being, akin to God, which puts him into a category entirely different from the animals. In the purely physical realm we are not superior to the animals. It is in the realm of the spiritual that the difference is located. Listen to the words of Professor J. Y. Simpson, in his volume *Man and the Attainment of Immortality*, "But whatever the place of man in nature be, he is distinguished as man from the rest of the animal creation by his knowledge that he has a place in nature, by his discontent with life on a purely animal plane, by his power to communicate his ideas in speech and writing to his fellows, by his ability to fashion tools, and by what may be termed his capacity for God—in short, by a whole series of physical qualities, which makes it immediately clear that it is in his spiritual rather than his physical nature, however derived, that his real significance lies."[1]

---

[1] Reprinted by permission of George H. Doran Company, publishers in America.

The evolutionist is much more cautious to-day than he was a generation ago. He thought then that the process was about unraveled and that he might soon tell how it all took place. But further study has shown that he really knows very little about it, that connecting links are missing, that he cannot prove how the development from the simple to the complex took place. All he now feels completely justified in claiming is that all the indications point toward enormous reaches of time during which very gradually what we now see around us was coming slowly into its present form. He is able to give a reasonable explanation of a surprising number of the factors, but at several points of great significance he must acknowledge ignorance. He cannot account for the emergence of life nor for the rise of the human mind and soul. All he can do, if he be a Christian, is to acknowledge that God's ways are marvelous and beyond our ken. This does not prevent further study as he reverently attempts to find out God's ways, but it does make him more humble and less confident of discovering all the secrets of God's handicraft in making the marvelous universe which lies open to his gaze.

Two other matters may be briefly considered. One is that the meaning of the whole long process as far as we can interpret it to-day is that God intended to produce men who were free and therefore could look forward to immortality, immortality here being interpreted as fitness for fellowship with God himself. With a wonderful sweep it is possible even for us men to get some conception of what God may have had in mind as he initiated the process and now continues it in his wisdom. The one supreme aim is to bring forth men who shall choose to be like Jesus Christ and thus put a capstone on the whole edifice. It is not an aimless evolution toward nothing in particular, but one in which a purpose is being worked out, a purpose so lofty and wonderful that we shall not be able to ascertain its meaning until we shall have been changed into the likeness of Christ and shall be able to interpret the meaning of his coming to the world in the light of God's whole purpose for men. When that revelation shall have been appreciated, it may be we shall see that everything in the universe points toward one end, the production of a race of men and women who in the immortality to come shall be able to have fellowship in that great family of divine love which shall continue to exist through the eternities around the throne of God. If this should prove to be the end of creation, it may seem to us that even the long ages of the process may be but a few moments, and that, after all, the one great factor is that God initiated it all and carried it through in order that an end which he thought was worthy should come to a marvelous consummation.

One last item should surely not be forgotten, for it seems necessary if we are to look at the question of evolution from behind as well as from before. Studying what the evolutionists now say, it is quite evident that they do not claim that evolution is an endless process, coming to no conclusion. It does actually reach a climax. It did so in the person of Jesus Christ. No one has ever superseded him. Evolution reached a limit and produced its ideal of morality and religion when it produced him. He was God's gift to the world. He entered into the human process and gave us something of its meaning. The meaning of the process is to be interpreted by Jesus Christ. All that we are and have, all that we hope to become is a part of God's plan that ultimately we shall be like him as we become more and more partakers of the divine nature. This is the end toward which the process has been moving from the beginning, and Jesus Christ stands out as the great indicator of its meaning. We may to a certain extent enter into that meaning and think the thoughts of God after him as we try to understand the purpose he has had in mind in producing so fair a universe.

CHAPTER V

HOW DOES GOD MAKE HIMSELF KNOWN?

It is the problem of revelation—how does God make himself known? In approaching this question it is well to call attention first to the persistent and universal belief that God makes his will known in such a manner that men can ascertain it if only they know how. The word "God" has been used here, but before speaking of the revelation of God as we know him in Christianity and one or two other higher religions, we ought to discover how deep are the foundations of the belief in the religious life of all peoples. What we find is that every religion, no matter how simple or confused its teachings may be, has believed that it is possible to come into contact with and find out something about the higher powers and their will for men. There have been many methods used, all considered effective even when failure ensues. Failure is caused, not because the will of the gods is impossible to discern, but because men are stupid and have not learned how to read the signs by which the spirit world sends its messages into the world of men.

The methods of divination are about as numerous as the kinds of religion in the world. The very word "divination" itself is significant. The attempt in each case is to find out what the Divine Being has in mind and what message he has to convey. In ancient Babylonia the attempt was made to find out the will of the gods by a process called hepatoscopy, or the reading of the god's will by observation of the liver of sheep. The liver was chosen because it was thought to be the center of life. It contains more blood at any one time than any other of the organs, and they believed that the "blood is the life." The sheep was chosen because its liver has more convolutions and presents more different aspects which can be observed and studied than the livers of other animals. So when the chosen animal was opened and the liver observed more different things could be read from the liver of the sheep than from any other animal. Literally hundreds of rules were deduced, by the use of which it was thought possible to determine what the gods had in mind to do or to allow among men. For the time being—and this is very important to remember—the god identified himself with the sacrificial animal, so that by reading the signs on the liver of the sheep the very will of the god could be determined. As Professor Jastrow remarks, we are actually looking into "the workshop of the gods" when the sacrificial animal is opened and the liver carefully observed. In other words, the gods reveal themselves to men in such fashion that, when men have been trained to read it, their will is made plain to people here below.

In Babylonia, where divination flourished as in few other lands, another favorite method was by the pseudo-science of astrology. Out of astrology grew the modern science of astronomy, but the two are very different in aim. The old priest-astrologer in Babylonia believed that divine beings were identified with the stars, and, if only he were able to read the stars correctly, he would be able to find out the will of the gods for men. A part of the theory was that our little world here below was a miniature of the great world of the heavenly bodies above, and that what happened here was absolutely determined by the movements of the heavenly bodies. If only, then, one could read what the starry heavens and the gods who were identified with them had to say, we could be altogether sure of what was to take place in the world in which we live.

One of the favorite methods of reading the will of God has been the casting of lots. We may go into almost any part of the world and find instruments for casting lots, the belief being that, since the falling of the lot is altogether uncertain, it must express something beyond human wisdom, even the will of the gods themselves. Scholars are of the opinion that in the old Testament the Urim and Thummim were instruments with which the lot was cast. We find that in the New Testament the early followers of Jesus cast lots to determine who should be the successor of Judas Iscariot. The present writer remembers hearing an ordination sermon in the Moravian church in Bethlehem, Pennsylvania, in which the bishop who was conducting the service said that he would preach from two texts, one the text which he himself chose, the other the text which had been found by use of the lot. In every case the attempt is to discover the will of God, for God will make his purposes known to those who have learned the secret of revelation.

Divination has been practiced in other forms, as, for example, through oracles such as that at Delphi in ancient Greece, where the Oracle sat on a tripod above a rent in the ground through which it was supposed that some divine being conveyed answers to the questions which men and women brought to the temple. Even among ourselves dreams and visions are considered means of revelation, whereby something is given to us by higher powers of which otherwise we would be ignorant. The will of God has been looked upon as conveying itself to man in ecstasy and even in drunken delirium. We still call strong drink "ardent spirits," which harks back to the time when it was believed that the intoxicated man had not only lost possession of himself but was in the possession of the spirit who was attempting to reveal some truth through the incoherent words of the half dazed man. This has been true in India and among the Shamanistic worshipers of northeastern Asia. Many are the means by which men have tried to find out things which were normally beyond their vision and their hearing. One of the most common methods, particularly in the higher religions, is to look upon the sacred book or books as containing a revelation of the divine powers. So we have the ancient Classics of China, the Vedas in India, the Avesta among the Zoroastrians, the Koran among the Mohammedans, the Holy Scriptures of the Old Testament among the Jews, and the Bible, containing both the Old and the New Testament, among Christians. All of these in one way or another are looked upon as sacred because they are thought of as containing a revelation of God.

What shall we say of this persistent belief that God makes himself known to man and that man can understand the revelation? It is universal and always has been. Principal Fairbairn stated it thus: "Of every religion revelation is an integral part; the man who does not believe that God can speak to him will not speak to God." So then the possibility of religion involves the possibility of revelation. So important is this feature of the religious life of man everywhere that without revelation we would not have religion at all.

We must not allow the puerilities of the means used to find out the will of the gods to lessen in any way the force of the testimony which comes from their use that men believe that God makes himself known. But at the same time the strange and to us irrational means of divining the will of the gods must cause us to ask whether in many cases these men and women were not wrong in their expectation as to what they might find out. This becomes very evident if one gives himself, even for a short period, to a study of revelation in the history of religion. As men increase in intelligence they drop one after another the more irrational methods, but so long as they are religious at all they continue to believe in revelation, which they can read and interpret.

We may now approach the question from the standpoint of our own religion. What is it God has been all along trying to impart and is still imparting to man through the process of revelation? Is it the communication of certain truths in science and history and ethics and theology, truths which the human mind could not otherwise reach? Is there not a clue just here? May we not say, and say it reverently, that, if there were any other means to discover and appropriate truth, God could scarcely be expected to interpose a special or specific revelation in order to do for man what he could in course of time do for himself? Let us remember that formulated truth is always a human product and must be. If it were not, it could not be assimilated by us at all. One of the most helpful of all the pedagogical principles which are now controlling the world of education is the principle of apperception. According to this principle we are able to interpret and assimilate only that truth or only those facts which can be definitely related to the body of fact which we already possess. New truths and their assimilation are definitely conditioned by what is known as the "apperceptive mass," or, in other words, the degree of development of our minds at the moment when new facts are presented to them. When any one comes into contact with that with which he can establish no relationship, it is almost as if it did not exist for him. If he thinks about it at all he is in utter confusion. Only when his development has proceeded to the point where what is presented can be brought into recognizable touch with what is already there, can it be used at all. Only then is there an accession of real knowledge.

This can be applied directly to revelation in the religious sphere. All truths must be so presented that they relate themselves, with some degree of familiarity at least, to what already is known and is being put into use. Then it becomes a part of our knowledge, and out of it may grow new attitudes toward life. As soon as we study the Christian Scriptures we are able to appreciate this fact. In the early day the revelation of God differed from the revelation in the New Testament. The very doctrine of God itself changed during the centuries, as did the doctrine of the future life and of sin and salvation. Jesus gives abundant evidence of this when he says that certain things were given in the past because of the hardness of men's hearts. But now, since men were able to appreciate it, it was possible to present truths which could never have been understood before.

All this leads to the conclusion that our best course

is to seek to find in revelation not formulated truths, which change from time to time, but something far more fundamental. What could that be? What is the very center of Christian revelation? The thing which we wish to know above everything else and which is absolutely necessary if we are to be brought into helpful relations with the universe in which we live is God himself, his nature and character and purpose. In Christianity the conception of God has been a growing one, with ever new revelations of his will and character. Every Christian who appreciates the significance of his life finds that he is on a great and wonderful quest, and that God's Spirit speaks to him in many ways, so that he has an ever fresh realization of the meaning of God as his experience develops.

For those who have ears God speaks and reveals himself in various ways. Undoubtedly the heavens declare the glory of God and the firmament showeth his handiwork. There is a revelation of God in the very creation itself, in the nature which surrounds us. For the reverent mind a study of nature is an attempt to understand God, and God does marvelously reveal himself to those who are in accord with his purpose and who are humbly attempting to find out his ways in the many forms of life which are spread out on every side. It is impossible to doubt that there is a revelation of God in man himself, in his ideals and aspirations and in his conscience, where the voice of God grows strong and can be heard as distinctly as the deep bass tones of an organ even in the midst of music which is being produced in the higher registers. The Old Testament shows us that there is a revelation of God in history, for, if the history of Israel means anything, it lies in the fact that God was revealing himself in all the vicissitudes of the history of that wonderful people. We need not, however, confine ourselves to what is known as "sacred" history. All history becomes sacred when we begin to realize that God shows himself to be what he is in it. God is surely revealed in great religious characters, in prophets and seers, in preachers and teachers, in parents and friends. God reveals himself in men like Moses and Elijah and Isaiah, in Paul and Peter, but who would hesitate to say that he has also revealed himself in Augustine and John Calvin, in Martin Luther and John Wesley, and even in later times in such glorious characters as Dwight L. Moody and Henry Drummond and Phillips Brooks? Every book-lover who has attempted to read the meaning of life in the world's literature feels perfectly sure that he has learned something about God in great books. There can be no doubt that the secret of joy in reading consists partly at least in the revelation of God which comes through the pages of the great writers of drama, the epic, and the higher fiction. Above all, the Bible stands out as the great classic of the world's religious literature. Here we can listen and discern the voice of God more clearly than in any other books that have been produced. This book gives us the truth concerning human nature and God and the relationships between them better than any book that has ever been penned.

But after all this has been said the distinctively Christian note has not yet been sounded. God has revealed himself as he is and finally in Jesus Christ, our Saviour and our Master. God has been revealing himself through great personalities, but here is the supreme personality of the ages. In other personalities we get only a partial vision, very slight in most cases, but here in Jesus Christ we see God as he is, expressed in human form. The supreme wonder lies in the fact that human nature is capable of such elevation that through flesh and blood there can come to us in language that we can understand and in acts which speak even louder than words such an intimate view of God that, when we have seen Jesus, "we have seen the Father," as Jesus himself said. God reveals himself "in divers portions and in divers manners," but once, as the climax of it all, as the author of Hebrews put it, he has revealed himself in a Son. As a Son he bore the very image of God himself, and as one who was a human being he revealed God in terms which ordinary men and women might understand. God has revealed himself as he is in Jesus Christ; that is one of the supreme facts in our religion, if not the supreme fact itself. This it is that makes it a distinct religion and causes it to stand out as unique in comparison with the other religions of the world.

This brings us specifically to the Bible. The question has been asked, Is the Bible a revelation or is it the record of a revelation? In other words, do we have the revelation in the history of Israel, in the prophets, and in Jesus Christ, or in the book which preserves the record? I really do not feel that the question is as important as it has been made to appear by some. It does help us, however, to see where the emphasis ought to lie, and, when we approach the question from the standpoint of emphasis, there can be no question that the essential revelation lies in history and in personality rather than in a book. Yet we must hasten to state that without the record, without the book, we would be helpless. The Bible is essential because it conveys to us who live long after the events recorded what is of as much value to us as to those who were close to the events themselves. The book is of prime importance if Christianity is to continue through the ages and if we are to be able to propagate it to the ends of the earth. But with this priceless book in our hands we must never allow its possession to blind us to the fact that the real revelation is through the history and the personalities of which the book is a record. It may truthfully be said of Judaism and of Mohammedanism that they are book-religions. There have been many who have made the same statement concerning Christianity, but there is a very real difference. Christianity is not primarily the religion of a book. It is in the first place and supremely the religion of a person, Jesus Christ. Christianity *possesses* a book,.and without it we would be paralyzed, even if we could ever have become Christians at all, but the emphasis is forever to be placed on the person. Our religion is the religion of a person, whose record is given in a book. This is the true order. We are glad, then, because of the Bible, for it presents Jesus Christ, but the gift which it bears is even more precious than the casket in which it comes. The Bible lifts up Jesus Christ and hence it is of incalculable value. But the Christ who is lifted up is the object of our faith and the supreme revelation of God whom we worship and adore.

We need to realize the wonder of this gift which God has made of himself in Christ. We are told that in him "are all the treasures of wisdom and knowledge hidden" (Col. 2. 3). We are still unable after the centuries to reach the limits of meaning which lie hidden

in this revelation, for when our ears are in tune we
find that some of the hidden things become known
and we discover more far-reaching meanings in Christ
than those who have gone before. It was John Rob-
inson, the pastor of the Pilgrims in Holland, who
said that there was much knowledge yet to break
forth from God's Word. This is supremely so when
we come to Jesus Christ, who in certain senses is well
known but in others still lies hidden from the eyes
even of his own followers.

CHAPTER VI

IS THE BIBLE GOD'S WORD?

By biblical inspiration we mean that we have in the Bible a book which has its source not solely in the minds of men but in the will and purpose of God. It is called "inspiration," or "in-breathing." God, in other words, breathed into the minds of men what they were to convey to their fellows, and we have as a result the Holy Scriptures.

We have just studied the subject of revelation, or God making himself known. And now we take up the counterpart, or man's side of the process by which the revelation of God is understood and made known to man. As Professor Marcus Dods puts it, inspiration is "the human qualification for understanding and recording revelation." Thus far the way is fairly clear, but when the attempt is made to define more exactly what is meant by inspiration we are in difficulty.

Let it be realized that other religions claim inspiration for their sacred books, and in some cases have theories of inspiration far more thoroughgoing and drastic than the most extreme view held by Christians. The best illustration is that of the Koran. The orthodox view which has been held down through the centuries by the Mohammedan teachers is that the Koran is the uncreated Word of God, that it has always existed as a finished product at the right hand of God on high. When Mohammed arose, God, according to his predetermined purpose, made the already existing Koran known to the Prophet. It came in bits, long and short, as Mohammed needed it from time to time. What we have to-day in this volume, which is about as large as the New Testament, is a book in the Arabic tongue, which, it is claimed, never had an origin but is eternal in the same sense that God is eternal. It was never written but had always existed, and was communicated by Mohammed as it came to him through the various means which were used to put the words into his mind. There is nothing in Christianity which goes quite so far in its claim as this orthodox theory of inspiration in the Mohammedan religion.

There are those, however, in the Christian Church who make the claim that the Bible is almost as completely inspired. They speak of it as "plenary" and "verbal" inspiration. According to this theory every word in the Bible was dictated directly by God. The writer was only a pen, one might say, held in God's hands. Some have been foolish enough to declare that even the vowel-points in the Hebrew text were dictated by God, not knowing that the vowel-points were invented by the Massoretic scholars only in the seventh or eighth century of our era! The result of this claim is that the Bible is said to be insured as a unique divine product. It is thus made absolutely inerrant in every statement and infallible on every subject it touches directly or indirectly. Much more might be said concerning this very thoroughgoing doctrine of inspiration, but surely this is sufficient to indicate that there are scarcely any loopholes left for any effective human element to be found in our Scriptures. It is true that the theory is not held in so complete a fashion by many, but it is better here to present the extreme view in order to make clear what the theory of plenary, verbal inspiration really means when it is consistent with itself.

Even these extremists, however, have not been able to escape the presence of certain discrepancies. When these were discovered they had to do something, and they fell back upon the theory that if only we had the original documents these at least would be found absolutely faultless. The discrepancies, they claim, had crept in through the carelessness of copyists in the days before printing was introduced, when it was very difficult to see to it that every copy was exactly the same as the original. This is a very strange claim in view of the fact that the original manuscripts have been lost, and lost beyond hope of recovery. The oldest New Testament document now in existence only goes back to the fourth century after Christ, and the oldest Old Testament documents are several centuries younger. We are in the situation to-day as if they never existed; they give us no help whatsoever. If God by the miracle of verbal inspiration provided an inerrant text, it is very difficult to understand why he did not by the same power provide that this text should be faultlessly preserved. An inerrant original is perfectly useless to us, and what we have to do with are copies in which mistakes and discrepancies undoubtedly are to be found. If an inerrant text were as indispensable as an original miracle on God's part would seem to indicate, it seems strange that we through the ages should be compelled to use a text which is not in conformity in every respect with the faultless text of the original documents. The fact is, the whole theory is impossible and falls to pieces.

It is built up to sustain a theory and does not rest on facts. It is an illustration of the danger of *a-priori* reasoning, starting from what one thinks inspiration ought to be, and building up a theory on that foundation, irrespective of many facts which should be taken into consideration. What we ought to do, in all fairness to the Bible, is to go to the records themselves without a theory and discover the kind of book the Bible actually is. Then it is possible to arrive at some theory which comes out of the study of the facts themselves, and which adequately accounts for the facts which we have discovered.

When we do this what do we find? It is with no sense of trying to find difficulties that the following paragraph is written. The only desire is to help the student to understand some of the factors which have entered into a theory of the inspiration of the Bible different from that just presented. A number of examples could be given to show that the New Testament writers were very inaccurate in their quotations from the Old Testament, that there are different narratives of the same occurrence which do not exactly agree with each other in both the Old and New Testaments, that the words of Jesus are given differently and are set in different circumstances by the evangelists, and that the various writers give ample evidence of having written as the writers of other literature go about their task. We are told in the first four verses of his Gospel that Luke wrote, "having traced the course of all things accurately from the first." He also gives ample evidence that he had taken into consideration the many narratives which he found describing "those matters which have been fulfilled among us." Judging from this preface, the conclusion we would reach is that Luke went about his writing very much as a scientific writer of history would do to-day. There is no evidence that he felt any necessity resting upon him to write in a different fashion. We have in the Bible quotations from other literature of a more or less secular character. There are many evidences of candid human testimony with no coercion determining from the outside what should be said. In fact, the pages would be spoiled, so far as our ability to ascertain the truth is concerned, if these men who spoke in the Bible did not speak out of their own experience without any outward compulsion whatsoever. These and many other facts have led men to see that it is impossible to hold that the Bible is a dictated book. This does not in any sense destroy its inspiration. It does, however, make it exceedingly difficult, if not altogether impossible, to hold to the theory of verbal inspiration and an inerrant body of scripture which resulted from it.

When these statements have been made we have scarcely touched the real problem. When a book is as precious as is the Bible, it is no pleasant task to pick out discrepancies. They are there, and we must study them at times, but we would greatly prefer to keep our minds fastened on other factors which raise the Bible to the highest pinnacle among the sacred books of the world. The great fact which stands out most clearly when the Bible is read is that we have here a book with God in it. As Samuel Taylor Coleridge has it: "How do we know this book came from God? I know it because it leads me to God. No other book does that in the same way, and therefore no other book is inspired as is the Bible."

This approach suggests a question which **may**

trouble the thought of some who are trying to be
consistent in their thinking. Suppose other books
lead me to God? Are they inspired or are they not?
I do not think we should hesitate a moment at this
point. Can any other conclusion be reached than that
any writing which leads us to God and to duty and to
thoughtful consideration of our fellow men is an inspired writing, in so far as it accomplishes those ends?
I do not come to the Bible with a theory; what I am
glad to do is to lay it down by the side of other books,
many of which have influenced me profoundly and
have led me to God. When I do this I make a wonderful discovery: that the Bible, in a sense which is true of
no other book, makes God known most consistently
and most clearly, wakes up the human conscience, and
teaches that men are brothers the world over. No
literature can compare with the Bible in this supreme
quality. It is inspired in a sense which can be said of
no other book, and yet I am profoundly thankful for
the other books which lead me to God and help me
to think of him and of my duty.

On this same principle of comparison I find great
differences in the Bible itself—that is, in this quality
of leading men to God. The only conclusion I can
reach is that there are great differences in the inspiration of the various writers. There are many examples
of this. Surely, no one could claim that the book of
Esther is to be compared for one moment with the
book of Psalms, or that the book of Chronicles stands
on the same level with the prophecies of Isaiah. Even
in the New Testament there are differences of level.
When one reaches the summit of revelation as it is
to be discovered in the Four Gospels, he finds himself
at a lofty height, and actually looks down upon other

levels, which, when brought into comparison with books outside the Bible rise supremely above them, but when compared with the Four Gospels seem not to be able to lift the human soul to heights quite so sublime. Our very use of the Bible proves conclusively that in practice some books do more for us than others. We have our favorite passages, and here and there in both the Old and New Testaments pages have been worn thin by frequent usage. Thumb-marks in the Psalms and in the Gospels give ample evidence that here is where many have found God as in no other places in the Scripture.

Another important consideration must now be noted. This varying library of writings has a real unity, a unity leading up to a grand climax in the record of the life and teachings of Jesus Christ. In such a building, to change the figure, all kinds of material must be used. One material is much more essential and precious than another, but in the Bible we are led to feel that the books hang together, that each part is appropriate, and that the very climax which we reach in Christ causes us to be thankful that the lesser writings are there, for each has some contribution to make to enable us to appreciate the meaning of the final revelation which has been made in Jesus Christ himself.

Another question emerges, if we are to be consistent in our view of inspiration as given in this study. How does it happen that in the Bible we should have an inspiration different from the inspiration of the great characters of the early church, or of prophetic preachers and writers to-day? This question is not difficult to answer. It must be remembered that the saint who lives to-day does have a kind of inspiration, the very real kind which leads men and women to God. All we have to do is to compare the results to-day with those achieved by the saints of long ago to be convinced that all inspiration is of a piece. And yet there is a very great difference between those who speak to us out of the Bible, particularly the New Testament, and all other prophets of God since their day. At least one element in that difference is that the men who wrote the Bible, especially those who wrote concerning Christ, were very close to the fundamental facts of Christianity. Only one set of men in all the history of the world could give us what these men have provided. We have these sublime pieces of literature, not necessarily and only because these men were greater or even more completely inspired than other men who have lived since, but because these men, mediocre men in many cases, lived with Jesus and felt the glow of that personality and had the unique opportunity of putting it down in imperishable Gospels which will go on influencing the lives of men and women as long as the earth lasts. The great theme of the Bible is Jesus Christ. These men knew him and have given us the great classic of religion in this book which deals at first hand with him. We draw on this source because it brings us into the closest contact with the basal facts on which our faith depends. Even in the Old Testament the sublime heights which were reached by Isaiah and Jeremiah and others were possible because, in the midst of the tragedy of the day in which they lived, their minds and hearts were filled with the promise and the glow of a better day, and they felt they had a part to play in making ready for that time. This, too, could happen only once in the history of the world, and we are profoundly thankful that such men as these were present and were able to record the meaning of the events through which they passed and the meaning of the vision which came to them of the Messiah that was to be.

And now to sum up in just a word: men are inspired, not books. Inspiration would seem to mean a heightening of the human faculties so that God and duty are seen more clearly. The "inspired book" is the record of what such men spoke or put down in writing. They saw clearly and wrote it out in their own words and in their own style and in their own thought-forms. They were children of their own times, even though they proclaimed a message whose inner meaning is true for us to-day. Thus we have the Bible. It is God's book in the sense that God spake to the men who wrote it and speaks to us to-day through these men who were inspired to give us his message.

CHAPTER VII

WHAT AUTHORITY DOES THE BIBLE POSSESS?

WHAT right has the Bible to command my intellect and my will? As one of my old theological professors used to say, the question of inspiration is of great importance, but cannot compare with the problem of authority. The final question to ask about the Bible is concerning its right to demand obedience on the part of men and women. Authority is a recognized fact in all the relations of life. Without it society would fall to pieces and government would be impossible. In the very lowest stages it is recognized as well as when men have reached the highest plane of civilization. It is not only true in the Christian religion, but in all religions. They would never be considered worthy of allegiance if they did not have power to command the mind and conscience of their followers. It is extremely instructive to a Christian to study the authority exercised over the mind of a Mohammedan by the Koran and the Traditions of the Prophet. They are the unchangeable Word of God to him and demand unquestioned and immediate obedience. The authority exercised in the Mohammedan religion works almost automatically. No Mohammedan belongs to or is a member of a mosque. There are no pastors who have authority to compel him to obey and to punish if he fails to do so. The Mohammedan society has so implicitly accepted the rule of the Koran and the Traditions that the young grow up with no other thought in their minds. It is taken for granted and is almost instinctive, but this does not prevent it from being effective in an almost absolute sense. The social pressure is so unconsciously exercised and yet is so great that a man would be as likely to break the religious regulations as he would be to take his own life. Here is authority to an almost unlimited degree.

The honor in which the Jew holds the Law and the obedience he gives to it furnish another illustration. To a greater or lesser extent the same thing is true of the other religions, and even down among the animistic peoples there is a rule which touches their moral life, and there are regulations which are to be obeyed in religious practices which are binding to an extent surprising to those who have never studied the life of these simple peoples. So we come to the study of the authority of the Bible with the realization that we are dealing with a world-wide phenomenon and not something which appears in Christianity alone.

We may start with the theory still held by many, at least as a theory, that the Bible speaks the final and compelling word on every subject with which it deals. There is no limit imposed; the theory brooks no resistance. Since in the Bible God speaks, we are to disregard any statement made by anybody if at any point it conflicts with a statement found anywhere in the Bible. This is as impossible as it is simple and drastic. Even those who accept it in theory are compelled to deny it in fact. The Bible is built, so far as its theory of the universe is concerned, on a geocentric plan, but everyone who has any intelligence whatever to-day takes the radically different view that

the system of which the earth forms a part is helio-
centric, and that even our little system centering in the
sun is but a minute part of the great universe of which
we get a glimpse on a starry night. Many other illustrations might be used, but this is sufficient to cause
us to face a most important question, namely, Shall
we refuse to listen to the scientist and the historian
except when they are in exact agreement with the
Bible? The importance of this question cannot be
overemphasized. We may get one approach to the
attitude which certain people have by the story, probably fictitious, of the destruction of the library at
Alexandria at the time of the Mohammedan con-
quest. It is said that when the Mohammedan con-
queror was urged not to destroy this valuable collection of the learning of that day, his answer was that,
if the books in that library agreed with the Koran,
they were useless, and if they disagreed with the
Koran, they were pernicious, and so ought to be sent
up in flame and smoke in either case. Very few would
go so far as this to-day, and yet it is only the logical
outcome of a theory which is held in varying degrees
of intensity by many who are truly Christian people.

When once we see what is involved in any such drastic
theory, we realize that we are face to face with a real
difficulty. The devoted Christian man who believes
this is deeply perplexed. If the Bible is an authority
on some things and not on others, who is to draw the
line? Are we not in a most dangerous situation? But
with all the issues involved there is a way out which
has already been found and is everywhere applied.
There need be little difficulty if we realize what all of
us are already doing. It may be we have only to ask
a series of questions to discover that we are already

making very significant discriminations. Is there anyone who would say that polygamy is a good thing,
because David had many wives? Would anyone declare that the old doctrine of "An eye for an eye, and
a tooth for a tooth" is tenable to-day? Are we not
involved in contradicting the Scripture in our practice when we allow women to speak in our churches,
when we remember that this is contrary to a direct
and explicit command to be found in the New Testament? Other examples might be given, but these are
sufficient to show that we are already doing critical
work on the Bible even though it may be done by
most of us unconsciously. We make discriminations
by the exercise of our own human judgment, and are
compelled to do so. The consensus of judgment
among Christian people accepts the situation caused
by the demands of the hour and acts upon it. This is
not an unchristian thing to do. The very spirit of
Christ in the hearts of men causes them to take posi-
tions which were not dreamed of a few generations
ago. This is true of the position of women in the
family and the church. There are differences of interpretation in various Christian countries according
to the stage they have reached in the rise of woman
to a place of equality with man in their social life. We
feel the influence of this consensus of opinion and
more or less consciously acknowledge it. This means
that we have a monitor, a standard of what is right
and what is true, and we deliberately set aside what
is incongruous with that standard. We will not follow
what seems not to fit in with what we conceive to be
the Christian attitude at this point and that. What
we all want is to be sure that God has spoken. Whenever we are sure that it is God's will, we recognize its

authority over us. To be a divine command it must be congruous with what God has come to mean to us from the Bible and from Christ. There must be harmony between what comes from the revelation in the Bible and the monitor or conscience within. Retaliation, which is taught in the Old Testament, does not command our obedience because it is not in harmony with our conscience, which has been educated by coming into contact with the spirit of Jesus in the New Testament. Even on the theory that the Bible and the church are an absolute authority to us, we must never forget that this recognition goes back to the time of an initial act of private judgment on our part when we deliberately gave assent to the supremacy of the Bible, or, it may be, the church over our mind and conscience. The question may be asked, Is there nothing more objective than this? We must realize that the standard is that of the life and teaching and spirit of Jesus, and that should be objective enough. He gave us an example by saying that certain things in the Old Testament were not to have authority over us. What we must do is to live in the spirit of Jesus and to be so filled with the significance of what he thought and did that almost instinctively we come to the place where anything that jars with the meaning of Jesus Christ in our hearts is repelled and thrown out as being something incongruous or even dangerous to our moral and spiritual life.

That which we are asking here is that we openly acknowledge what all of us tacitly assume, and, having done so, to apply consistently this principle to the whole phenomenon of the Bible. The principle is stated very clearly by Professor Marcus Dods: "The only possible ultimate ground for believing Scripture to be the Word of God is that there is that in the truth delivered which convinces me that God is its author.'' We are not so convinced, however, when it comes to science and history, and many are being compelled to admit that what the Bible says concerning the earth and its creation and the movements of ancient history are not to be accepted as our authority in these matters. We can test out the fact that the earth is round and would have to throw away our reasoning if in spite of demonstration we should still affirm that the Bible is correct. What the Bible does is to register the scientific and historical attainments of that day, the day in which its several parts were written. Whether we like to admit it or not, the fact is we have made real progress in science and history, progress very far beyond the possibilities of knowledge which existed in the days when the Bible was written. Its statements cannot be authoritative for us unless they are corroborated by facts which have become established during the centuries. It would be flying in the face of what we actually know and act upon in our daily lives were we to do anything else.

Is the same thing true of everything the Bible contains? If so, we would be in a sorry plight indeed. We would surely be in need of a new Bible, as Mr. H. G. Wells and George Bernard Shaw suggest. When, however, we bring the moral and religious conceptions of the Bible to play upon our minds and hearts, the reaction is entirely different from that which takes place when we attempt to accept the scientific and historical statements of the Bible as authoritative, particularly those in the Old Testament. We come to realize that the Bible is not the same from beginning to end, but that, when we are able to arrange its parts chronologically, there is both a moral and a religious development. It is this development which is one of the most significant things in the Bible. It helps us to see how out of crudeness and inadequacy we finally reach a summit which is far higher than any plane reached by other moral and religious books. The Bible authenticates itself as a worthy authority over our mind and conscience. We have not superseded it; we are still following after with the gleam far out ahead and with no likelihood that the case will ever be different. Any Bible which a man might construct to-day must either base its teachings on the Bible we now have or immediately fall to a lower level in the estimation of all religious people.

Whenever we approach the Bible inductively the conviction becomes stronger the further we go that what God intended in his revelation was not to teach man many things which he might far better learn for himself, but to reveal himself to man, to show man to himself and thereby light the way back to God. The conclusion we should reach is that the Bible is an authority and has the right to command us on what God intended to make known, himself and man's relation to him. God did this supremely in his Son Jesus Christ our Lord. He is the supreme authority because we are most sure that in him we are in contact with the very mind and heart of God. In the Bible we have the record of this revelation and in varying degrees we are conscious that God speaks through its pages. In each case the test which must be applied is the Christian consciousness which has been built up through fellowship with and obedience to Jesus Christ, the supreme revelation and the test of all revelation.

CHAPTER VIII

HOW DID THE BOOKS OF THE BIBLE GET TOGETHER?

We take the number and order of the books of the Bible for granted in most cases without stopping to consider what right we have to do so. Might not changes be made in the collection of books which we call the Bible? Would there be any loss or any gain by doing so? The subject of the canon of Scripture is far more important than many Bible students recognize, and we ought to touch on it even in so brief a study of the Bible and Christian doctrine as we are attempting in this volume. About the only method available is to go back as far as possible to discover how the books of the Bible actually got together. We wish there might be more evidence, but such as we have sheds much light on the process, and furnishes a clue to the motives and reasoning of those who were responsible for the collection of books as we now have it.

The arrangement of books in the Hebrew Bible is quite different from the arrangement in our English translations. It would be very helpful for us to lay aside our English Old Testament for a time and study the Bible as it is in the Hebrew. It would doubtless teach us certain lessons about the books which can scarcely learn with them arranged as they are in the books we commonly handle. In the Hebrew Bible the Law comes first, as it does in our translations.

The Law includes the first five books of the Bible, the so-called books of Moses. By all odds they were the most important part of the Bible. Nothing else was considered comparable to these books in authority and in the love and veneration in which they were held by the Jewish people. Next to the Law came the Prophets. This section of the Bible included more and less than the books we speak of as prophetical. They included Joshua, First and Second Samuel, Judges, First and Second Kings, Isaiah, Jeremiah, Ezekiel, and the Book of the Twelve. The twelve small books of the Minor Prophets as we know them made but one book in the Hebrew Bible. It is very clear that the historical books were looked upon as prophetical in the same sense as Isaiah and Jeremiah. They were not such in the sense that they dealt with the future. They were prophetical in that through them God is thought of as teaching his lessons, lessons which come either directly through the word of the prophet who is supposed to have written them or through the history which tells of God's dealing with the chosen people. Finally came the Writings, which include the Psalms, Proverbs, Job, the Song of Songs, Ruth, Lamentations, Ecclesiastes, Esther, Daniel, Ezra, Nehemiah, First and Second Chronicles. It is significant that these four books which come last in the Hebrew Bible were not considered on an equality with the historical books which were considered a part of the prophetic literature. All the books, in fact, in the group of Writings were thought of as occupying a relatively inferior position as books of Scripture.

What is the meaning of this threefold arrangement? Doctor Skinner says that "the three divisions represent three successive stages of canonization." The Law was always held as the most sacred division by the Jews. The reason the historical books were included among the prophetical books is that it was thought that they were written by prophets, hence they could claim the same prophetic authority. The Writings were a miscellaneous collection which only gradually came to be accepted as canonical, and which could never be held in the same esteem with the earlier portions.

There was great difference of opinion as to certain books like the Song of Songs and Ecclesiastes, which, when the canon was being formed, were said by their opponents to "defile the hands." Esther and Ezekiel were also seriously questioned. On what basis, then, did these Jews decide on the canonicity of a book? It is somewhat surprising to know that the process, which was gradual, was not completed until only about a century before the time of Christ. Doctor Skinner mentions three principles which guided the Jewish leaders before the time of Christ in settling the problem of what books should be included in their sacred scriptures. The first was "conformity to the Law," that is, agreement with the first five books which were considered the norm by which the other books were judged. Then there was a certain time limit which was considered important. Only those books were to be included in the sacred book which had been written before the reign of Artaxerxes, who is the equivalent of the Ahasuerus of the book of Esther. The last one of these principles was that the books which were to be admitted must be written in Hebrew. This cut out the books of the Apocrypha, which at that time were circulated in Greek translations. They had been originally written in the Hebrew but had been translated and so were rendered ineligible to inclusion in the sacred canon.

When we come to the time of the New Testament we discover at once that the followers of Jesus simply took over the Old Testament as the Jews received it in their time. They asked no questions; they simply used it as their Holy Book. For some decades it was the only Bible they knew. Then certain books in the New Testament gradually superseded the Old Testament in the estimation of the disciples of Jesus. Finally, when the New Testament was complete, it was joined with the Old Testament to make the one Bible of the Christian Church.

The first part of the New Testament, that which earliest was recognized as authoritative, were those books which contained the teachings of Jesus. This process started long before the day when the Gospels as we have them to-day were written. But when these Gospels came into existence they were almost immediately looked upon as carrying the authority of Jesus himself. It was very clear that they took the Christian back to Jesus as could not be said of any of the other books which were submitted to the early church for decision.

Paul's Epistles at first were authoritative only to the church to which each was sent, but as they were passed around from church to church they came to be looked upon as of great value by all the churches. We do not know the exact process; we are only sure of the fact. By the end of the second century, and not until then, do we find a New Testament like our own. But when this has been said we must realize that differences in judgment relative to a number of the books were very freely spoken. Even books which were included in the canon in some parts of the church had to wait for several hundred years before they were received finally as a part of the collection which was binding and authoritative upon the whole Christian Church everywhere. The book of Revelation, the Hebrews, the second letter of Peter, and the Epistle of James had real difficulty to be included in the canon. Probably the book of Revelation was longer refused admittance than any other, some parts of the Christian Church holding out for hundreds of years against its inclusion. There was also another side to the forming of the canon. There were many who thought that other books ought to be included, but they did not succeed in making good their claim. Among the writings not accepted were First Clement, The Shepherd of Hermas, and the Epistle of Barnabus. These books failed to become a part of our New Testament, but were as strenuously defended as some of the books which were included. The weight of opinion, however, finally turned against them, and they are not in our Bible to-day.

Are we bound by the decisions made by Jewish scholars before the time of Christ and by the early church in their list of canonical books? The church, of course, settles the question officially for Roman Catholics. What about Protestants? It is very refreshing to find how free Martin Luther and John Calvin were in their judgments. Luther looked upon the Epistle of James as an "epistle of straw" and thought it ought not to be included in the canon. He was strenuously opposed to it because it seemed to him to contradict the general sense of Scripture in making salvation depend partly at least on works and not solely on faith. Only at a later time did Protestantism shut down on all freedom and demand that the traditional canon of scripture be recognized as authoritative. They wanted it to be settled once and forever. But what shall we say? The essential fact underlying Protestantism is that we are not bound by external authority. Every Protestant has the right to make his own canon by excluding books from the collection and including others which are not a part of the Bible. In one sense he does not exercise that right, but in another sense he is constantly working at the problem of his own personal canon. Whether he will or not there is a kind of canon of Scripture which each one makes for himself. We do not reason about it; we come to it unconsciously. Some books mean far more to every Christian than others. It proceeds much further than that; some books do not make an appeal and are almost as if they did not form part of our Bible at all. We may formally acknowledge the correctness of the decisions which have given us our canon, but the working canon, which is a man's real canon, is frequently quite different.

The whole question is one of religious experience in its final analysis, with scholarship playing an important but subordinate rôle. We must go to the experts and secure from them the best their scholarship can do to give us what they only can contribute, namely, facts concerning their origin and genuineness, the credibility of the narratives, and the closeness of connection with the great vital facts on which our religion depends. But in addition to this it is the sense of congruity with the total meaning of our religion as it is lived out by devoted men and women which is the final and decisive factor.

The question may arise, Is there anything outside the Bible which is more important to us than some things in the Bible? We need only to ask this question to answer it. In a very true sense every one of us has a Bible outside the Bible. How many of us place clippings and excerpts, poems and devotional sayings within the covers of our Bible and find ourselves going to them, not more frequently than we go to the Bible, but far more frequently than we go to many parts of the Bible, for spiritual help and encouragement. God speaks to us through them, and we read them again and again and are nourished and uplifted.

The reason for referring to this process which goes on in the experience of every devoted Christian is that it helps us to understand how the canon of the New Testament was originally formed. The Gospels were received because they brought Jesus close to the men and women who composed the newly formed church. The apostolic authority of Paul and Peter and John carried their writings into the canon. This was doubtless true of the Epistle of James. But while this motive was at work there was another which cannot be eliminated. The books which were gradually received as canonical satisfied spiritual need. They became more and more indispensable as men sought guidance and comfort and help. It was a moral and spiritual process, and we are the recipients, not only of the critical acumen of the early scholarship of the church, but of the spiritual intuitions of devoted men and women who found that these books ministered to them in a peculiar way. One book here and another letter there were cherished by a group and really were the Word of God to them, and when, after several centuries, the curtain rises, the canon of the New Testament as we have it to-day emerges. It had proved its fitness to meet the needs of the church, and that is its claim to our acceptance.

Some of us may not be entirely convinced. We might wish that several books might have been included which are now rarely read, but which have nourished the faith of many. Protestantism has gone almost too far in the estimation of many in not emphasizing the Apocrypha, as do the Anglican and Roman Catholic Churches. We may read it to our profit to-day. And the same is true of several Christian writings which failed of admission to our New Testament. But this may be said, there is no likelihood that it will ever lead to a conflict. These rejected books and epistles are available for any who may want them, and no one desires to hinder the fullest appropriation of their contents. What is patent, however, to those who have gone to these books is that they do not add any essential element to what we already have in our New Testament. All a Christian needs is these. We have to be profoundly thankful to the early church for giving us such a wonderful collection. It was collected and preserved and transmitted by men acting more wise than they knew, and we are the richer for it. All we have of our Lord Jesus Christ comes down to us in these precious documents, which have become to us the very Word of God.

CHAPTER IX

WHAT IS A MIRACLE AND DO MIRACLES HAPPEN?

WHAT is a miracle? Many would say that it is an act of divine intervention in human affairs which sets aside or upsets the laws of nature. If this is a correct definition, then we have our hands more than full. I think that in the end miracle, so defined, would be discarded by anyone who thinks and who appreciates the kind of universe in which we live. It is simply impossible for the scientist of to-day to believe that anything upsets the way in which the universe is conducted. We are coming very rapidly to the conception of a universe of law and order, not a capricious and untrustworthy universe. We may increasingly count on the universe and be sure of certain things about it. This makes impossible a conception of miracle as an event which contradicts the order of the universe, which is out of conformity with the laws of its working.

There is, however, a different definition which many seem to have forgotten, a definition which comes out of the distant past, enunciated by the great Augustine himself. He says that "a miracle (*portentum*) is not against nature, but against known nature." This changes the situation very materially. How much do we know about God's universe at best? Very little, and our knowledge shrinks when we begin to realize what a wonderful universe it is, as we see it through the eyes of intrepid scientists who are bringing things to light about it which were not dreamed of a few years ago. How unscientific, then, for any man to affirm that we know the universe so well that we can with confidence declare that nothing can happen which runs counter to what we at this time know of the laws which govern it. This is what a dogmatic denial of miracle really means. It is highly unscientific, as unscientific as it is to claim that miracles break the laws of nature. There must be more modesty on both sides—Augustine can help us even yet.

But what has been said does not carry us very far. The question arises as to the reason why certain things should be done contrary to what we are accustomed to in the world. Why should not God do things in the ordinary way, instead of occasionally performing an act which confuses us even more than the strangeness of what is ordinarily taking place in the nature around us? This needs to be stated with great care in view of the marvels which are performed by the control of nature which would appear miraculous to those who lived not very long ago. The true starting-point must be our belief in God as a personal God who is the Creator and Sustainer of the universe and everything in it. When we have such a belief we have already admitted the possibility of miracle. As Professor Wendland puts it: "Belief in miracle is connected in the closest way with belief in God. To believe in the living God and to believe in miracles are the same thing." What Professor Wendland evidently means is that a living, personal God should have as much liberty in his universe as his children on this planet. We can and do manipulate the laws of nature all the time. We set one law in operation against another and we initiate what would never have taken place without us. The universe in which we live is very freely acknowledged as plastic in the hands of God. He is working out his purposes and using the forces of nature to accomplish his will. Man is thus like God; he is producing effects in a universe which is plastic to him too. The world is a different place to-day because of what man has done, and the development was never so rapid as now.

In doing all this man is not running counter to the laws of nature. He is learning what they are and how to make use of them. This could only be done in a universe of law and order, in which it is possible to place absolute confidence that it will be true to itself. We cannot admit that God has less liberty in his universe than we have. The so-called "laws of nature" are his ways of working, and he ought to be able to use them for his purpose. God is still fashioning the world in which we live and doing it to the working out of his purpose. The world is not a closed system, but the expression of the will of a living, personal God on whom we may depend as we do on the rising of the sun every morning.

Still, if God is immanent in his creation, and if all that takes place is the expression of his will, why should he ever depart from the ordinary method, and do that which seems to contradict the normal working of his will? The sufficient reason is because he is not only immanent, but also transcendent and has a relation to his creatures which in his judgment at times demands special action, not contrary to nature, but using its forces in an unaccustomed way. One of the apt illustrations used by Doctor Harry Emerson Fosdick is that of an imaginary man whose house was near a railway. He tried to construct a time-table by noting the passing of trains. After a number of days he had worked out a fairly satisfactory schedule. He had been able to schedule the passing of trains and by this method had come to the conclusion that the trains were fairly regular. The whole thing, however, was spoiled one day by the passing of a train which had no connection whatsoever with the schedule he had been able to make out. He did not know what to do about it, but on making inquiry was told that it was a "special." Because he had been able to work out a time table on the basis of the ordinary running of trains was no reason why the superintendent of the road should not send out a special train when there was need for it. The scientist is very much like this man. He tries to discover the laws of God's universe, not by direct revelation, but by watching the effects and trying to record results, and in the end drawing conclusions from what has taken place. When he has done this and has verified it times without number, he is able to say that he has now discovered one of the laws of nature. We have come to look upon these laws as dependable, and in hundreds of cases our daily lives are what they are because of the dependability of nature in continuing to do what certain men have discovered were the laws of their operation. There would be no more incongruity, however, in something taking place which goes beyond the possibility of explanation than there is in a "special" on a railway.

A miracle, then, is a manner of dealing with nature and with man which cannot be accounted for by what we know, but which on that account is in no wise a violation of nature's laws. Wendland says, "The only things broken [in a miracle] and shattered are erroneous conceptions of law and causality." If I can do something of great benefit to you which would never be done in the wide world if you did not ask me to do it, we have the best of evidence that we do not live in a closed and rigid system, but one which can be used for the good of others. When we are doing many things to-day which would have been accounted miracles by men of a previous generation, why should not God be doing likewise? The fact is that every process of nature when closely studied leads us into mysteries and causes us to wonder, if only we push our inquiries far enough. Miracles differ from the ordinary workings of nature only in that we find ourselves at the end of our resources of explanation sooner than at other times. God seems to act more directly here than usual, and we are the more perplexed by it.

What has already been written does not settle the question, even though we may accept all the conclusions which have been suggested. We proceed but a very short distance before coming across such a statement as that of Matthew Arnold, "Miracles do not happen," and a large number agree with him. They have thrown over their belief in miracles entirely. These persons are not all outside the Christian Church. There are those not out of sympathy with the church who remain obdurate and who feel that they must be skeptical whenever anything unaccountable is said to have taken place. Their attitude is this, "Suppose all that you say be true theoretically: it is still impossible to believe that five thousand men were fed with a few little loaves and fishes." Goethe once said to Lavater, "A voice

from Heaven would not convince me that water burned
or a dead man rose again." Here, then, we meet
vigorous opposition to any theory of miracle and to
any attempt to show that the evidence is strong
enough to convince the inquirer that the biblical miracles actually took place. Even in the Christian
Church the situation is very different to-day from
that of fifty years ago. At that time miracles were
one of the most dependable evidences of the divine
origin of Christianity. Now, at the very best, miracles
are looked upon as themselves in need of explanation.
Instead of believing in Christianity because of miracles, about the only way we can believe in miracles
is because of their connection with Christianity, which
we have come to believe in on other grounds. Even
then many feel that they are not essential to Christianity at all and might better be quietly dropped
with no danger in doing so.

The student of biblical miracles to-day is forced to
come to a conclusion which would have surprised the
Bible student of past centuries. He finds it necessary
to distinguish between miracles. When he has accepted the belief that miracles are reasonable he has
not thereby committed himself to accept all the miracles of the Bible without further consideration. He
is bound at this point as at many others to study
sympathetically the evidence for each miracle or
group of miracles and to come to his conclusions on
the basis of the weight of evidence which lies back of
each. It is quite possible for him to disbelieve in this
miracle or that and at the same time be an ardent
believer in some other occurrence which is just as
miraculous as the one which he is unable to accept.
It is not a question of all or nothing. It is a ques-

tion of evidence, and each Christian has a right to demand that he be asked to accept nothing unless on the basis of evidence sufficient to bear the weight of the conclusions in question.

If it is a question of evidence, what kind of evidence must we demand? It would be perfectly useless to appeal to anyone to believe that a miracle took place unless there was in it a demonstration of goodness and beneficence. There are many who would say that a mere exhibition of wonder-working would not be sufficient to prove that such an occurrence took place. There must be a gracious design in what God does. It is from this viewpoint we must study the miraculous in the Bible today.

An illustration from the Old Testament may be helpful, even though the conclusion reached in this case is negative. We are told in the book of Joshua that at the battle of Beth-Horon the Israelites were successful in the battle, and that in order to complete the victory the sun and moon were told to stand still. They stood still and the day was prolonged and thus the victory was made the more secure. This is one of the most difficult of all the miracles in the Bible to accept because it involves movements in our solar system which would seriously upset the calculations which astronomers are able to make of that which seems to have been an undeviating process throughout long ages. We are very greatly relieved, however, when we discover that this statement in the book of Joshua is not an original statement in that volume, but is a quotation from a poetical book called the Book of Jasher. What we have, then, is a poetical account of what took place on that glorious day when the Israelites were so successful over their enemies, quoted from another book, but not necessarily to be accepted as literal fact.

Turning to the New Testament, we may consider the healing miracles of Jesus. It is impossible for us to deny that Jesus performed wonders which cannot be explained by what we as men can do. We can go farther than those of a generation ago, but we are unable to travel the full distance of complete explanation of what Jesus did. Much has been learned concerning autosuggestion and the influence of spirit over body and very accurate studies have been made of the miracles of Jesus from this standpoint; but when all the evidence is in, sane writers declare that there is still an unexplained factor which doubtless will remain inexplicable through the years. The reason for saying this is that so long as Jesus himself is inexplicable, it is not surprising to find he did works of the same character. The greatest miracle about Jesus is his moral character. A sinless Christ among human beings is a stranger fact than the ability to work miracles among men who cannot perform them. We must remember, however, that Jesus' own attitude toward miracles was very different from that of many of his defenders. He always seemed to hesitate about performing miracles, and sometimes performed them when prudence would have dictated a different course. We cannot find that he performed them for the purpose of proving his own claims. What he did was to work miracles out of a heart of compassion to help people who were in trouble. They were altogether congruous with his purpose. When, however, he talked about them, he seemed to intimate that his ability to work miracles did not differentiate him from his disciples. He declared that they would do greater works than these. He sent them out not only to preach, but to heal and to cast out demons. It seemed to Jesus that this power which he wielded came from God and that his disciples had recourse to the same power and could do the same works if they were able to exercise the faith in God which he had.

When this attitude toward the miracles is presented we begin to feel that there is another side to the whole question. It is almost impossible to escape the conclusion that Jesus intended his church to be a miracle-working church, and that we are falling short of our possibilities by not being able to do certain things which the gospel narratives show very clearly Jesus had in mind for his followers after he had left them.

And why should not this be so? Are we inferior to the early church? Have we less of the Spirit now than they possessed? Ought we not to be able to come into the same relationship with God that was experienced by the disciples of Jesus? It is very difficult to answer these questions without reaching the conclusion that we should make a renewed study of the whole question. It should be from the viewpoint that miracles are not isolated phenomena which occurred only at one time in human history and that they were completely to cease. It is true that from Jesus' statements it would seem that miracles were to play a secondary part in the work of the Kingdom, that the ministry of the church should be more concerned with matters of character and of spiritual influence than the ability to work what are commonly called miracles. Yet it is very difficult to read the words of Jesus and to study his relationship with his disciples without feeling that we ought to expect the same results to flow from our ministry which characterized his ministry and that of the disciples who followed him.

Do we realize that we usually consider the question of miracle as something which attaches to the Bible and the Bible alone? What is needed to-day is not only a theory of the miracles of the Bible but such a relationship to the real significance of miracles as shall make it possible for us to feel that we belong to the apostolic succession, and that there is nothing which we read of in the Bible which is not possible to a praying church to-day. The question is very difficult and has many pitfalls, as all know who are acquainted with the work of so-called faith-healers and others who are little better than charlatans, but this should not prevent us from coming to the study with fresh enthusiasm to try to find out what meaning the idea of miracle may have for our day. It may result in bringing us into closer contact with the apostolic age and in filling us with a new enthusiasm. Have we not been humbled by lack of power? Is there not much more healing potency in this world of ours than we have yet made use of? Do we realize as we ought what power we might wield if only we might learn again the secret of tapping the unlimited resources of God?

CHAPTER X

WAS JESUS CHRIST A REAL MAN?

WHEN we approach the question of the person of
Jesus Christ we have reached the very center of the
Christian faith. We call our religion Christ-ianity;
the most significant question which we can ask is,
Who was Jesus Christ? This is so important that we
should scarcely expect an easy answer. No answer
which is completely satisfactory has ever been given.
The difficulty lies in the fact that the Christian consciousness through all the ages has unequivocally declared that Jesus Christ was both human and divine.
How is it possible to think of one being who is both
human and divine at the same time? The danger
has always been to emphasize one or the other of these
two sides of the person of Christ, and by so doing to
minimize and sometimes even to disparage the other.
But with all the over-emphasis and the under-emphasis,
of which many illustrations can be found through
Christian history, there has been a tendency, whenever men have reopened the question in order to find
a more satisfying answer, to reaffirm what Professor
Mackintosh speaks of as "the fundamental assertions
of the Christian consciousness." The most persistent
of these age-long affirmations has been that just
stated, that Jesus Christ is truly man and truly God.
We cannot imagine how the Christian Church could
have originated or continued through the centuries
unless this conviction had been at the heart of it all.

Professor Burkitt, of Cambridge University, has made it very clear that the four Gospels in the New Testament would never have become what he speaks of as "the official charters of the church" had it not been for a kind of necessity which rested upon the early church to make sure that the followers of Jesus might never forget the true human nature of their Lord. This is somewhat startling to those of us who are living in a very different age, when the most frequent denial is that of the divinity of our Lord, and not of his humanity. And yet when one considers the full significance of the discussion it is a little difficult to decide which is the more dangerous of these heresies, the one which would deny the divinity of Christ or the one which would deny his humanity.

One of the earliest tendencies in the history of Christian thought, which we can scarcely say rose to the dignity of a heresy, is that of Docetism, the theory that Jesus Christ was not a real man at all but only seemed to be a man. He acted and talked as a man does, but this was really only acting a part. He was divine; that was what really counted, but he was able to act so much like a man that we are frequently confused and are actually led to say that he had a true human nature. This, however, is a mistaken conclusion. There was no real manhood at all. This tendency appeared even in the apostolic age. It was easier for men and women then to think of Jesus Christ as divine than it was to think of him as human. They raised him to such a lofty height that his humanity, his intimate fellowship with men, his real human experience, was in danger of being lost sight of. This tendency toward Docetism never assumed the same definiteness as did other heresies which were combated and eliminated from the main current of historical Christianity, but it has always been present as a tendency and we find it with us at the present time.

In approaching the study of the person of Jesus Christ, what has already been said makes clear that we must discover what our original data are. And when this has been done there can be little doubt that the final facts with which we deal are to be found in the four Gospels. What we discover there is, first of all, a man who walked with his disciples through the fields of Galilee, a man who taught the people by the seaside, a man who went to his death in Jerusalem, and, we must not forget, one who rose again and appeared to his disciples. Whatever else we may come to in the course of our study, this is the necessary starting point if we are to preserve our sense of reality and remain on solid historical ground. We need to realize that this is the way the disciples of Jesus traveled. They came to him in the beginning with no doctrine of his person, with no theological theory as to who he was. They followed him, as was customary in the East, as a religious leader who interested them and who they felt was worth following. It is doubtful if there was any more in their minds than that another prophet had appeared, one who after a long period when there had been no prophets, might be proclaimed as another in the honored line who would speak out God's message again to his people. Then as they journeyed with him this human being began to take on proportions which surprised them. Their own minds were enlarged as they lived with him and they began to see more in their leader than they could account for on the basis of sheer human nature. In the end they did a very strange and unheard-of thing. Monotheistic Jews as they were, intent above all else upon doing honor to God and not blaspheming his name by according divine honor to other beings, these men were in fact led to treat Jesus in the same way in which they treated God and accord him the same kind of worship which was due to Jehovah alone! And they did this with no sense of incongruity; it seemed the most reasonable thing they could do.

I do not know of any other way by which we may arrive at a doctrine of Christ's person, which shall be at once scientific and true to all the facts in our experience. We must walk with Jesus as his disciples did. This means that we must become acquainted with him through the four Gospels, and if we are to arrive ultimately at any complete doctrine of the person of Christ, it must be by journeying with him and allowing him to make his own impression upon our minds and hearts. This result cannot be reached by sitting down and coldly thinking it through; it must come out of experience and out of life as well as by reason. Many have made a mistake at this point. They have thought they could solve this problem as they do a problem in mathematics, by reason and by reason alone. It is true any doctrine we accept about Jesus Christ must satisfy our intelligence, but the approach must be through life as well as thought, through experience as well as reason.

This mistake has very frequently been made, of thinking that Christian doctrines are matters to be settled by the intellect alone. They never have been so settled in the past and they never will be. A Christian doctrine is the attempt to make clear to the mind what has been experienced in the broader reaches of human life. Only those who have experienced the influence of the living Christ upon their lives are competent to deal with so important a question as the doctrine of his person. We must come to the four Gospels and allow them to exercise their full influence. We may have no theory when we start except that Jesus is worthy of study, but it is quite likely that we shall have the experience of the first disciples. As we follow him in his teaching, in his relationships with men and women and with children, in his converse with God, in his self-sacrificing devotion to man, and finally in the climactic experience on the cross, we may be led to feel that there are many things there which make him more than a man for us. That is the typical experience of Christian men and women. But whatever else may be in our minds at the end, from first to last we must keep our feet on the solid rock of historical reality. Jesus Christ lived among men as a man, and whatever human traits we find exhibited in the course of his life of really human experiences are to be taken at their face value and not as the attempt on the part of a really Divine Being merely to make it appear that he is human when in reality he is not. With this in mind let us go to the Gospels, very briefly of course in such a study as this, and see what characteristics are displayed by Jesus as he lived his life among his disciples and the people of Galilee and Judæa.

He had a body of flesh and bones as we have. He was hungry and had to eat; he was tired and needed sleep; he became exhausted and sought rest. In no respect did he differ from us in the physical features of his life. When men lived with him they lived with him as a man, one who seemed perfectly at home in our world with its needs and its physical limitations. It would be possible to go through the Gospels and pick out many passages in which these characteristics are clearly exhibited, but we can only refer to them here.

He felt the same emotions we feel. He took delight in little children. He sympathized with men and women in their gladness and sorrow. He was deeply grieved when he found his friends in trouble. He knew anguish of soul and felt it deeply when those on whom he had counted failed to live up to his expectations. He drew back from death, hoping for a time that the dreadful cup of death on the cross might be removed from his path. We know that in the end he prayed, "Not my will but thine be done," but it was only after an inner struggle caused partly at least by the horror of dying a felon's death on a cross. He knew what it was to be utterly indignant, and we are told that he made a whip of small cords and drove out the money-changers from the court of the Temple, God's house, which he looked upon as a place of prayer and which they had turned into a market place with the desire to find gain for themselves. He also desired human sympathy, and when it came to the hour of anguish in Gethsemane, he took Peter and James and John a little farther into the garden with him that he might feel their presence near at hand. This desire for the comfort of their presence is pointedly expressed in his reproachful words, "Could ye not watch with me one hour?"

Jesus grew and developed not only physically and mentally, but in his moral and religious life. We are told that he increased in wisdom and stature and in favor with God and man. This means that there was a time when he was immature, when he did not see the light as it afterward dawned upon him, that he could not appreciate what in a few years was natural for him to see with the increasing experience which comes through the years. Reference may be made particularly to the experience when he was baptized by John the Baptist. The significance of that experience lies in the inner consciousness which came to him that in a peculiar sense God was his Father and he was the Son in whom the Father was well pleased. If he had not needed this experience it would not have come. We must by all odds save the sense of reality in the gospel narrative. This experience was not in the nature of theatrical acting but was a genuine experience which really met a want in the mind and heart of Jesus, something which up to this time had not come to him and which he needed at this point in his experience.

It would be very difficult to account for the temptation of Jesus had it not been for the revelation which had come just before at the time of his baptism. The revelation was so striking and so new that it was necessary for him to retire into a desert place to think through in the presence of God the meaning of what had taken place in his inner life. The same may be said with reference to the transfiguration experience. It came, not as a mere exhibition for the sake of the disciples, but because Jesus had reached a point in his experience where a revelation or a new insight was needed. It seemed to give him the encouragement and provide the interpretation which would carry him through the terrible experience of the months which were just ahead. One of the most common experiences of our Lord was in connection with prayer. Why did Jesus pray? Is it not necessary for us to say that he prayed because he needed to pray, because it was necessary for him to set aside other engrossing interests in order that the communion between himself and God might never in any manner be hindered? He lived his life in communion with the Father as a necessary condition of his development, in all this paralleling the experience of men and women who are trying to live with God to-day.

His intellectual outlook was the normal outlook of the men of his time, even with its limitations. Time was when such a statement would have been looked upon as heretical, but, thanks to the work of devoted scholars during the last generation, we have come to see the possibility of making it with no trepidation. It is now commonly held that the only way to protect the integrity of his character as a real man is to believe that there were limitations which even Jesus could not transcend. There could be no true incarnation without it. For God to be incarnate, to become man, implies limitation. This is so in the very nature of the case, and not because it is brought in from the outside and tacked on as an afterthought. When a woman came up from behind and timorously touched the hem of his garment, he asked who it was that touched him. He asked the question because he did not know and wanted to find out. He said very definitely on another occasion that he did not know the time of the coming again of the Son of man, that it was hidden from all except the Father himself. If we study the life of Jesus carefully from beginning to end, we shall discover that he lived the life intellec-

tually of the men of his time, that he did not anticipate any of the discoveries of modern science, that
he gave no indication of knowing anything about
what would take place when certain great scientific
discoveries should have been made or about the con-
stitution of the universe. What we need to remember
is that if it had been otherwise, he would have been
entirely out of touch and sympathy with the men
and women with whom it was necessary for him to
live. It is because he fitted in so perfectly with the
life that men and women then lived that we may feel
the touch of the eternal in his relationships. He
found men just where they were and understood them
completely. Our confidence that he is able to do the
same with men and women of our time is that he did
it perfectly with the men and women with whom he
lived in Galilee. Had he gone one step in advance and
talked about things which were strange to his con-
temporaries there would have been a touch of the
unnatural, of the uncanny, of the strange about it,
which would have alienated him from living contact
with human life as he actually found it.

Jesus Christ was tempted as we are, yet without
sin. We shall speak more of the sinlessness of Jesus
at a later time. The emphasis now must be placed
upon the reality of his temptations. I think of an
incident in the life of one of my friends who appeared
before a committee of business men in one of our
larger cities to be interviewed concerning the acceptance of a position of responsibility in the religious life of the city. One of these business men
propounded the question, "Do you think Jesus Christ
could have sinned if he had wanted to?" Is it possible to imagine any viewpoint further away from

moral reality than that? The implication in the question was that, even if he had wanted to sin, it would have been impossible because he was the divine Son of God and therefore was lifted above the plane occupied by men and women as we know them. Letting alone the utter psychological abnormality of such a conception, what we have to consider is that it reduces the temptations of Jesus to mere stage-play. If he could not have sinned, there was no real temptation, and yet it is stated very clearly by the writer of the book of Hebrews that Jesus Christ was tempted at all points like as we are. The lesson we were to gather from that statement is that we may find sympathy and help in the midst of our temptations because Jesus passed through temptations which were real and did it successfully.

We are quite likely to confuse temptation with sin. A sentence from Professor Mackintosh is as suggestive as it is true, "Sinless temptation may be the most severe." The conscience of anyone who has resisted temptation is more sensitive than the conscience of one who has failed to resist. The corroding and warping influences of sin have made it more difficult in that case to detect the evil in many suggestions which are not entirely black, but which are tinctured with evil sufficiently to reduce life to a lower level if we accede to them. But Jesus was one who felt the force of temptation more than anyone else could, for from his youth up all the evidence leads to the conclusion that in him we find the one absolutely spotless soul in all history. Yet in making this statement we must never fail to realize that his character was not a mere natural product, but a spiritual achievement, which resulted through the resistance of all the suggestions to evil and the consistent and reiterated choice of the best at every point where the necessity of a choice came before him. In this necessity he was truly a man, although in his sinlessness we begin to realize what began to dawn on the disciples, that they were dealing with one who was so far beyond them that it would be impossible for them to realize in their own experience what was most obviously an achievement in his. This thought will occupy our attention again; just now we must keep his humanity in view, so that we may realize that we have one who can deeply sympathize with us in temptation and lead us out through his example and strength into the better way.

When we say that Jesus was a real man we do not imply that he was or could have been greater than all men in every phase of human life. One writer has suggested that in philosophy Jesus could have surpassed Socrates, as an orator he could have eclipsed Demosthenes, and we might even go on and say that as a chemist he might have gone beyond Pasteur, and as a writer might have surpassed Shakespeare, and so on, but we gain very little by any such vain imaginings. Jesus was a real man and consequently could not have had all skill in everything. He was a typical man and not a prodigy. If we could think of one who could surpass all the men who have been pre-eminent in different fields, we would not have a human being at all, but a strange kind of monstrosity, whom none of us could recognize as closely related to human kind. One of the most suggestive passages in the New Testament is the one which expresses the surprise on the part of the people of Nazareth when Jesus' fame began to be noised abroad, that their fellow townsman was making a name for himself. They could not realize that the Jesus who had lived with them during his maturing life could be anything more than one of the ordinary villagers. Their exclamation was, "Is not this the carpenter and are not his brothers and sisters here with us?" If Jesus had been what the extravagant pictures of many would lead one to suppose, he could never have lived his life in Nazareth without causing not only his neighbors and his own countryside but the whole land to re-echo with the plaudits of the startling and strange genius who had appeared in their midst. The facts, however, are very different. He was a typical human being and lived his life among men like his fellow townsmen, causing no special stir among them.

This is not for one moment to intimate that the inner quality of the life of Jesus did not differ from that of his fellow townsmen during these hidden years in Nazareth. It would be impossible to conceive of the Jesus who spoke the parables and who gave himself to suffering humanity as being on the dull level of the residents of a little town in Galilee. They would have been amazed had they known the thoughts he was thinking and the purposes which were gradually forming in his mind. What has been said merely calls attention to the fact that the real differences between men are the differences of the inner life. Unless neighbors are very keen in their appreciation of real worth, a great spiritual character may walk in and out among them without calling the attention of the ordinary man and woman to the fact that there is one among them very different from themselves. All the evidence we find in the Gospels leads to the conclusion that Jesus Christ was a typical man and lived a life which was so nearly like the life lived around him that men and women were surprised when he began his ministry to find how he talked and what wonderful things he did. If Jesus may be spoken of as a genius at all, it is in the realm of morality and religion. Here he is unique. No other religious leader has ever appeared who can be compared with him here. He touched life at its deepest. He knew human nature as no one who has ever lived knew it and because of this it was possible for him to accomplish results which genius, showing itself at any other point in human life, could never have achieved.

But why this insistence on the reality of Jesus' manhood? Why should we not say that we have in him the divine Son of God without speaking of the fact that he was also the Son of man? Simply because we must be true to all the facts if we are to realize what the incarnation really means. If God did not fully partake of our nature in Jesus Christ, then there was no real incarnation. It would still be impossible for us to know what God is like unless expressed fully in a real human life. But if we hold that Jesus was truly human, all that God meant to convey to us is conveyed in human terms, the only terms in which we could understand God at all. The truest statement and the deepest we can make concerning the inner meaning of our religion is that God is like Jesus Christ. In Jesus Christ we see God in terms of our own experience. We may with reverence say that in Christ God looks out on human life through human eyes, that he speaks with a human tongue, that he acts through a human body and knows the facts of human life through human experience.

We may come closer home than that. Were Jesus

Christ not truly human he would not be our Brother and could not be our Example. Were he a being suspended midway between divinity and humanity it would be mockery to urge that we follow his steps. Only a being with his feet solidly planted on the ground, who thought our thoughts, shared our weakness and limitations, was tempted as we are, and was in need of going to the same source of moral and spiritual strength, could lead us to God. We shall come to see that we must not fail to maintain the doctrine of the divinity of Jesus Christ, but, before we are ready for that supreme affirmation, it is necessary to realize clearly that the being who was divine was also human, that his divinity did in no sense eclipse his humanity, that for any statement about Jesus Christ to be truly Christian humanity must be asserted as clearly as divinity. If this is not done we run the danger of losing the full wealth of our unique Christian heritage.

I do not know how better to close this study and introduce the next than in the words of J. S. Hoyland in "The Fourfold Sacrament,"

> "Christ,
> Most perfect man,
> And therefore perfect God:

> "Christ,
> Most perfect God,
> And therefore perfect man."

CHAPTER XI

HOW MUCH MORE THAN A MAN WAS JESUS?

In Fosdick's *Manhood of the Master* is a list of certain qualities Jesus possessed. Among them are mentioned the Master's joy, loyalty to his cause, power of endurance, sincerity, self-restraint, fearlessness, and affection. Why should these human traits be listed here when our task is to find how much more than a man Jesus was? Simply because we need constantly to be reminded that this is the only firm foundation on which any superstructure can be built. This is where we must take hold if we are to get a real grip on the facts, even on the facts of Jesus Christ's divine character. But having gone as far as we have, undoubtedly an objector might feel he had something to say. You have made Jesus so truly and completely human, where is the more-than-man, if any? I think this question is altogether justifiable and needs to be treated with the deepest respect. If the foundation we have laid is to be the foundation of a superstructure that is worth while, it should be tested in order to discover its strength and any possible weakness it may have.

But the very question which is thus raised frequently indicates that there is present in it a deep and fundamental misconception, a misconception into which the defender of the more-than-man conception falls about as readily as the detractor. It is the mistake of thinking that when one says a thing is human it cannot be divine, and when again a thing is divine it can have nothing human about it. This may be put more directly by saying that there is no reason why Jesus, who was a real human being, might not at the same time be divine without denying his humanity and without any essential contradiction in statement. There is an old idea which still persists but which is pagan to the core. It is the idea that whatever is really human is contaminated to a greater or less extent. We must admit that human nature can descend to a very low level, but that is not all. What of human nature at its best, above all in Jesus Christ? What does it mean that God created man in his own image? May we not add that with all that sin has done the divine image has not been effaced from human nature and that the touch of the divine is still upon us? The human at its best irradiates the divine. It is close to divinity itself, and it never completely loses that touch no matter how low it falls. So when we have thus made Jesus completely human we have in no sense lessened the possibility of divinity. The truth is, if we are to find the divine in Jesus anywhere, we may find that the only place where it may be discovered is right in among these qualities which make him truly human. But why should we want to go any further than the truly human? Do we not have enough in Jesus as a Brother and as an Example? What richness there is in Richard Watson Gilder's verse,

> "If Jesus Christ is a man,—
> And only a man,—I say
> That of all mankind I will cleave to him;
> And to him I will cleave alway."

---

[1] Reprinted by permission of Houghton Mifflin Company.

I suppose the only answer that can be given is that facts are very stubborn things, and there are some very significant facts in this case which cannot be avoided. What are these facts? The answer which would have been forthcoming at one time was that Jesus performed miracles and that these were evidences that he was divine. The change from this viewpoint has been rapid and striking. Instead of looking on miracles as helpful evidences of the divinity of Christ, they are looked upon almost as an incumbrance at the present time. If we believe in the miracles at all, it is because such a person as Jesus performed them. They do not stand on their own feet, and much less are they considered able to bear the weight of proof of the divinity of Christ. If we study the Gospels with care, particularly the first three Gospels, we shall discover that Jesus made far less of miracles than his followers have done through the centuries since his time. Not only is this the case; Jesus seems to indicate that his own disciples were to be empowered to do the very things he had been doing. There was in his mind no essential difference in this regard between himself and the disciples. They were to go out and perform miracles just as he performed miracles. If that be the case, it is very evident that, if the miracles of Jesus prove his divinity, the miracles performed by the disciples might be expected to do the same for them. This, of course, makes argument useless, for no one would think even for a moment of placing the disciples in a class by themselves, separate from the rest of humanity.

If miracles do not give us the help we need, to what facts shall we turn? It seems clear that if we are to find evidences of his divinity, these evidences ought to lie in the region of the inner life and of character. In other words, they ought to lie in the realm of the deepest things in human life, the things which determine the character of one's life more than any other factors could. It is here that we begin to realize how inadequate the argument from miracles is, for at the most they could only prove that Jesus was a worker of miracles, or, to put it in other words, a wonder-worker. If he were not more than that, we could scarcely speak of him as being our divine Lord and Saviour. .Even the miracle of the virgin birth is scarcely able to bear the weight which is frequently placed upon it. We may admit the strength of the argument on which it rests, as many of us do, but even then the New Testament itself does not justify us in using it as a kind of final proof of the unique nature of the person of Christ. It does not stand alone. It appears in its beauty only when we think of it as the birth of Jesus, the Jesus whom we have come to love and reverence because of what he said and did and was.

Again we come back to the same facts with which we have been dealing, the human qualities which are indubitably a part of the life of Jesus, to discover what they have to give us. Another objector may be heard at this point. He would probably say that if this claim of ours can be substantiated, what we have really done is to make Jesus different from ourselves only in degree and not in kind. It may only place Jesus above us, and not over against us on the God-side of the universe. Here is a point of great difficulty and of great importance. We must look at it closely. In the first place, let us remember that a difference in degree if carried far enough is as significant as a difference in kind. In fact, it is the only kind of difference with which we can come to some understanding. If Jesus is so utterly different from ourselves that there is nothing essentially alike in him and ourselves, there is no possibility of our understanding him. Those who are claiming so insistently that Jesus is different in kind from ourselves are actually putting Jesus further away from humanity than they put God. For if God created man in his own image, that can only mean that there are essential points of likeness between ourselves and God. Were it not for this it would be impossible for us to use any human analogy by which to convey to man information concerning the kind of God we have. We are in the habit of speaking of the attributes or qualities of God in human terms. What we mean to assert when we say that God is omnipotent is that he possesses power as we possess power, only to a degree which we cannot even imagine. When we say he is omniscient we mean that he knows as we know, only his knowledge takes in all facts in one intuitive grasp, which goes beyond the possibility of our understanding. It would mean nothing whatsoever to us if knowledge in God did not have some analogy with knowledge among men. All we are asserting about Jesus is that if we are to understand the deepest things in his character, we must find them in the realm of characteristics of which we have some appreciable knowledge through experience. Jesus was altogether sinless, but we too know what it means to overcome sin. Jesus was love incarnate, but we also know what it means to love, and the more we love the more we stand in awe and wonder at the love which Jesus had and which we cannot attain.

The question must arise whether in making this statement concerning Jesus we mean to indicate that in all points he is like unto ourselves without any essential difference at any important point. My feeling is that this statement could be made of Jesus no more than it could be made of God. We are made in the image of God, but God made us; we did not make God. In much the same way we might say that the character of Jesus has its analogy in our characters, but that we are dependent upon him for the development of what we have while he is not dependent upon us for that which makes him what he is. He is, as Professor Drown says, "the Creative Christ." We are the recipients, he is the Creator of character. He is on the God side of the universe. From him comes all the power which makes it possible for us to live the Christian life. We are on the man side of the universe and are helpless in ourselves, depending upon his bounty to accomplish the results which we so much need in order that we may be more worthy of our calling in Christ.

Let us look, then, at Jesus as we find him in the Gospels and discover what the appeal to his disciples was, which led them to treat him as their Lord and Master and eventually to reverence him even as they did God himself. He spoke with authority. His message and his personality were unique and compelling. Bishop McConnell frequently speaks of the "inevitability" of Christ. All men are different after they have come into understanding contact with him. This is true to-day just as much as it was with the throngs to whom he spoke in Galilee. Wherever the teachings of Jesus are carried they have become almost at once the standard by which men judge them-

selves. This is true in both Japan and China, where
the Confucian ethics have been the rule of life for
over two millenniums. When men in these countries
who are alert to the great movements which are taking place in the world judge other nations and individuals both among their own race and among
foreigners, the tendency is to judge them not by the
Confucian standard but by the Christian standard. It
is a very remarkable thing that in India not only Mr.
Ghandi but other less well-known leaders in Indian
thought are constantly judging their own acts and
thoughts and purposes by the standard of the gospel
of Christ, rather than that of their own religious classics. Jesus speaks with authority. There is an orig-
inality about his message which makes it unique and
separates it essentially from even the highest of the
ethical systems which have been promulgated in all
the ages.

His practice went beyond his precept. In this Jesus
is unique. The best comment on his teachings, that
by which we can learn more than is contained even in
their verbal statement, is his life and deeds. In this
he is in striking contrast to other teachers, who are
not slow to confess their inability to live up to their
ideal. Jesus went beyond his own precept in the
perfection of deed and life which characterized his
relationship with men and women. I have put it in
this positive way, which I believe to be more satisfactory than to speak primarily of his sinlessness.
Sinlessness is a negative quality. The wonder of
Jesus lies in the fact that he went beyond negative
sinlessness to the great positive outpouring of his life
in service for others, the perfect demonstration of a
love that went to the uttermost. As a positive force

for good he rose above any who have ever lived upon our earth. We cannot even imagine anything better than is disclosed in the Gospels.

He is unique among the world's lovers in his boundless compassion. We often teach the story of the feeding of the five thousand with the thought in our minds that the great difference between Jesus and his followers is that he could perform miracles and they could not. Ought we not, rather, to teach the parable thinking of his compassion rather than his ability to work miracles? It is at the point of his unselfish devotion to the men and women and children who were needy that he outstripped his disciples and left them far in the rear. It is a little difficult sometimes to appreciate this viewpoint. In such a case the best thing for us to do is to study what the great saints have had to say, Saint Francis of Assisi and others who have gone further than other men and women in their devotion to the good of mankind. When we go to such and ask them whether they have overtaken Jesus, the testimony is always that the farther they have gone in their devotion the farther Jesus seems to be out in the lead, exhibiting a devotion and compassion which increasingly becomes less possible for them to emulate.

He was perfectly at home in the spiritual world. His communion with God was unique. He lived with his Father on terms of intimate communion and fellowship. Do we realize how striking this is? Peter and the other disciples were orthodox Jews, believing in prayer and familiar with it in practice, yet when these men traveled with Jesus and watched his prayer life through the months they were with him they were led to realize how little they really had.

The end of it all was that they came to him and said, "Lord, teach us to pray." They realized that he was with them, eating and drinking and sleeping, and yet he lived a life of which they knew very little. He had food to eat they knew not of, and Jesus woke in their lives the desire for the spiritual communion to which he was habituated.

These are all traits of human nature, but carried to such a point of development that the disciples were irresistibly convinced that while they were dealing with a real man, they were dealing with one so far beyond them that their most exalted thoughts of the Jehovah of the Old Testament did not surpass the thoughts which were borne in upon them by their contact with Jesus. It was all expressed in human terms, because Jesus was truly human, but it could not have been more divine if God had done it himself. That was the actual conclusion they reached, that Jesus was a genuine incarnation of God, that he was God in human life, that when they were in touch with him they were in touch with Deity itself. The result of it was that they looked upon him not only as an example, but also as God manifest in the flesh, truly man and truly God in man.

It is here that the resurrection of Jesus Christ appears in all its glory and wonder. The same Jesus who lived with his disciples was raised from the dead and appeared to his disciples so that they could recognize him and have fellowship with him. But even more wonderful than this, Jesus gave evidence of his living presence in their midst after he had bidden them farewell. They knew he was alive even though they could no longer see him. This was the experience not only of the early disciples but it has been the continuing experience of all Christian men and women even down to our own time. As the writer of the Epistle to the Hebrews has put it, "We have not an high-priest who cannot be touched with the feeling of our infirmities." It is the present tense which is significant. Jesus Christ now lives, the God-man, raised to the right hand of the eternal God and yet at the same time retaining that essential humanity which makes it possible for him now to reach down, not only in power but in sympathy to lift poor sinful humanity up to himself.

Up to the present point we have been dealing with the primary affirmations of the Christian consciousness. There is a further question, however, which will not down and which must be faced. How are we to conceive of a divine-human person? In attempting to answer this question we must leave the field of experience and enter that of theory and speculation. We find the heart throbbing with fresh life which has come through an experience of contact with Christ, and we immediately find ourselves trying to justify the experience and explain it in intellectual terms. We feel the necessity to construct a theology so that the mind shall be satisfied, as well as the heart. It must not be thought that we can separate the two functions as distinctly as might be implied from what has just been said. It has been necessary to speak of them as distinct functions, but there is always the danger that the construction of the theology may become so far removed from the actual experience that it becomes very dry and abstract, of little use in explaining the facts of a vitalizing experience. But this should not deter us from the attempt, because as far as possible we want the intellect to be carried and be satisfied with an explanation of what has taken place in the form of an experience in the inner life. This does not mean that we shall arrive at a complete explanation. It can mean very little more than the removing of contradictions and pointing the way to that which through experience we may enter more deeply as we see into the meaning of what we have already discovered.

The great body of Christian men and women through the ages has held that Jesus Christ was an incarnation of God. God came down and lived with us as a man so that we were able to see God in terms of human experience and life. It was God manifest in the flesh. God was in Christ reconciling the world unto himself. We must be very careful in our use of language at this point. Looking out of a railroad window some years ago I saw a large sign and on it was written in very plain letters, "Jesus Christ is God." I must say that with all my conviction of the divinity of Jesus Christ this sign grated on me. I have thought of it many times. Did it tell the whole truth? Was it not attempting to overdo a great truth? Jesus Christ was God; I believe that, but is not something more needed? He was God, but God manifest in the flesh, and when you state that other side of the truth you realize that in becoming flesh certain things could not be said of Christ which could be said of God in all of his majesty on high. Jesus Christ was a real man, and in order to be truly human it was impossible for him to possess qualities which are those of the omnipotent God. I cannot help but feel that some kind of "kenosis," or self-emptying, was necessary. We read in Paul's letter to the Philippians that Jesus Christ "emptied himself." This means that certain things could not be said of him as he lived his life on earth which could be posited of the Divine Being himself at the center of the universe holding all things in his authority.

The demand may be forthcoming that a very exact statement should be made at this point. But in the very nature of the case it is impossible. We do not know the process by which the Divine Being found it possible to be manifested in a human life. We are in ignorance. Something had to be laid aside, but not everything, simply because humanity and divinity are far from being exactly alike, although they are not completely separated from each other. If there had been a complete disparity, there could have been no incarnation. If there had been no laying aside of qualities such as omnipotence, again there could have been no incarnation, for man is not God even though he shares his nature.

Down through the Christian centuries, ever since the Council of Chalcedon in 451, an explanation has been made which has been looked upon as the official doctrine of the Christian Church. This Council declared that Jesus Christ was one single personality, but this single personality consisted of two natures, one human and the other divine. It is almost impossible to hold this doctrine to-day. It seems perfectly inevitable to a student of psychology that, when we say any being has two natures, there must be two streams of consciousness, and that is so abnormal and even so impossible that it must be rejected by anyone who would win the approval of thoughtful men. There is no evidence for this in the Gospels, and they are the final court of appeal. Very frequently we have heard men say, "Jesus did this by his human nature, and that by his divine nature." All such statements are superimposed upon the gospel story and did not come out of it. Whatever Jesus did, whether it might seem to be human or divine, appears to come from the same personality, in which there is no division of natures. His is a unified personality with no cleavage that makes itself evident in any statement that can be drawn from the Gospels. If we have learned anything from recent study, it is that we can make no progress unless it be based on the declaration that in Jesus Christ we have one personality, one human-divine nature. It is not two natures, the one human and the other divine. He is our divine Lord, but at the same time he is the man Christ Jesus.

This Jesus Christ of whom we have been speaking is the revelation of God. This is the supreme affirmation of Christianity. He revealed God as he is because he was so connected with God that when we look at him we know what God is like. What was the nature of this connection with God which makes it possible for him to reveal God, which makes it possible for Paul to speak of Christ as "the very image of his substance"? I do not think this question can be answered to our complete satisfaction. It has been tried many times. The Greek theologians of the fourth century declared that Jesus Christ was of the "same substance" as God the Father. But that does not carry us very far to-day. Put into our own language it would seem to say that Jesus Christ shares or actually is that which makes God essentially what he is. This is undoubtedly true, but is not the kind of truth one knows how to use. The only thing of which we can be sure is that when we look at Jesus we are led to the conviction that we see God as he is.

There need be no hesitancy in speaking of the deity of Jesus Christ as well as his divinity. We see him in human terms to be sure, but that is the only way we could understand him at all. God, in other words, could not be more godlike than he appears to be when we see him in Jesus Christ. So marvelous is this possibility that there is no wonder that men and women have been led to fall down in wonder and open their mouths in praise that such a privilege should be theirs, that here in Jesus Christ they may see God and are able to come into effective contact with his love and wisdom and omnipotence. He is divine, he is God manifest in the flesh.

CHAPTER XII

IS THE HOLY SPIRIT A NECESSARY
REALITY TO-DAY?

WE read about God in a book, and believe he exists and that he is the Creator and Sustainer of the universe and everything in it. We read about Jesus Christ in the same book, and are led to put enough confidence in him to take him as Saviour and Master and model our lives after his example. Is there anything more? The Christian Church has always declared that there is.

Where shall we begin? We may take the statue of Phillips Brooks at Trinity Church, Boston—he stands there at a pulpit preaching the Word, but just back of him with his hand on his shoulder stands the Christ. Phillips Brooks was conscious of a Presence in his life and in his work, and his consciousness has been duplicated in the experience of ten thousand others from the day of Pentecost down to the present time. When they are most alone they are not alone. When they are in danger or in need they realize the nearness of an unseen Presence; they can do all things through an invisible Influence which energizes them. Could there be stronger testimony than this?

But others besides those in direct Christian activity have had a similar experience. "Sir Ernest Shackleton, like so many of the great explorers, was a strong believer in the nearness and friendliness of the Unseen Power. He was a mystic who was conscious of Another present with him in the white and lonely spaces. Of this experience of his he made no secret. Others might reason and welcome, he knew that the Unseen Friend was with him."[1]

Followers of Christ in all ages have claimed that they have been conscious of something more than the impulsion which has been conveyed to them by a book. They have testified to a prompting which is objective, but which has operated upon them from within. They have testified times without number that through this influence they have been shamed because of sin, drawn to what is better and higher, received the sense of assurance that they were forgiven and were members of God's family, been given direction in times of crisis and in the daily round, and have experienced a new dynamic which has made it possible for them to do what would have otherwise been beyond their strength. There are many differences in the way in which this influence is said to operate and make itself known, as many differences as there are different individuals who share it. But there is unanimity at one point: all testify that it is something objective to themselves and that it comes from God. They have asserted with confidence that they are having dealings with God through his Spirit.

We are compelled to admit with reference to so delicate a matter that the possibilities of error are great, that many of the so-called leadings and inner monitions which claim to come from God could never emanate from that source. He would be rendered absurd in many cases. When, however, everything has been said from the standpoint of the danger of error it is far from being a complete explanation. We must

---

[1] Reprinted by permission of The Christian Century.

remember that the claim is universal among Christian people and that it is made by many whom we are compelled to look upon as the best and sanest and wisest of the men and women who have accomplished results in the kingdom of God. We might far better conclude that mistakes do not prove that there is no correct reading of God's will than that all these men and women have been laboring under a delusion. It is necessary to make careful discrimination between this and that claim, but this is a very different procedure from throwing it all over as the result of a disordered imagination. We are never to judge of the correctness of such a testimony because we ourselves have never passed through a similar experience. This may be the result of our incompetence and lack of development in the things of the Spirit and the inner life. It may be that we have a total misapprehension of spiritual realities, and to judge others as being mistaken is really a testimony to our own spiritual immaturity. There are specialists and experts in the realm of the spiritual as there are in other fields of human life and activity. There are men and women who see clearly what others fail entirely to appreciate or see very vaguely or dimly in the far distance. It is surely the wiser policy to go to the experts in cases of this kind than to allow our own dullness to dictate what decision we shall reach upon a claim so wide-reaching as that of the presence of God's Spirit in human life.

Is there any standard which may be set up by which it is possible to test these inner experiences? How is it possible to differentiate between what is merely subjective and what is of God? We are very fortunate in having at least one criterion which is objective enough to determine with precision the character of the experiences which men and women claim to have had. Jesus set the standard for all such experience when he said that the Holy Spirit was his Spirit and it would testify of him. Here is something tangible and objective. Whatever else may be said about the influence of the Spirit of God in human life, it must be consistent and congruous with Jesus Christ. Otherwise it is not the genuine working of the Holy Spirit which Christians claim has influenced their life and conduct. The monument to Phillips Brooks in Boston rings true at this point. The influence which he felt in his ministry was to be identified with that of Jesus Christ. When Phillips Brooks sought to explain what took place in his experience the only satisfactory account was that which led him to see that it was a prompting identical with that exerted by Jesus on his disciples, the record of which we have in the Gospels. Thus everything may be brought to the touchstone of historical fact. It is not any influence which men feel which may be identified with that of the Holy Spirit of God. It is only that influence which fits in completely with what we know of Jesus as he walked and talked with his disciples in the pages of the New Testament.

Let us realize how closely this harmonizes with the promise made by Jesus. "Lo, I am with you always, even unto the end of the world. . . . Where two or three are gathered together, there I am in the midst." Paul, who was one of the earliest followers of Christ to share in the experience of the Spirit, spoke of it in these words: "It is no longer I that live, but Christ liveth in me." So, then, the first fact to keep in mind with reference to the Holy Spirit is that it is the Spirit of Jesus Christ in the world influencing men in what they say and do. Jesus made this very plain: "But the Comforter, *even* the Holy Spirit, whom the Father will send in my name, he shall teach you all things, and bring to your remembrance all that I said unto you" (John 14. 26); "But when the Comforter is come, whom I will send unto you from the Father, *even* the Spirit of truth, which proceedeth from the Father, he shall bear witness of me" (15. 26); "Howbeit, when he, the Spirit of truth, is come, he shall guide you into all the truth: for he shall not speak from himself: but what things soever he shall hear, *these* shall he speak: and he shall declare unto you things that are to come, . . . for he shall take of mine, and shall declare *it* unto you" (16. 13, 14). In other words, what Jesus did the Spirit does. So close is this identity that we cannot distinguish the work of one from the work of the other. But at all times we touch hard on historical fact when we are able to check up whatever is claimed to be the work of the Holy Spirit by comparing it carefully with what we have recorded of Jesus in the four Gospels. This means that in prayer, in the midst of temptation and trial, in the decisions we have to make, in meditation and in our daily conduct, a true Christian is conscious that he is being helped and that while he cannot see Jesus he knows that it is his Lord who takes him by the hand and guides him along the way. He never saw Jesus in the flesh, but it is as though Jesus himself were leading and speaking to him. He can account for his experience only in this way.

So important is this influence which draws the Christian on to holiness and nobility of character that it is even more important than the physical presence of Jesus himself with his followers. It was Jesus who made the declaration that, "It is expedient for you that I go away; for if I go not away, the Comforter will not come unto you; but if I go, I will send him unto you. And he, when he is come, will convict the world in respect of sin, and of righteousness, and of judgment" (John 16. 7, 8). Why was it expedient that Jesus himself should be withdrawn from his people? The faith which is necessary to see him who is invisible demands more inner development than seeing the physical Jesus. It was true then and it is true now. A physical return of Jesus to this earth would be no great boon, because it would localize Jesus instead of enabling him to have a universal influence equally present wherever Christianity is preached.

We begin to realize the great importance of this fact when we compare ourselves with the original disciples. How great was their opportunity in being able to see and talk with Jesus face to face! We are certainly at a disadvantage, a very serious disadvantage, were it not for the doctrine of the Spirit. Where there is this experience of the Spirit there is also a realization that we are no whit behind the original disciples in opportunity. We are not increasingly handicapped as the centuries pass as we otherwise would be. The living Christ is with us through his vitalizing Spirit just as truly to-day as when he talked to the disciples along the wayside in Galilee. We may summarize in the words of John Caird: "There is a presence of Christ with his believing followers infinitely more intimate and profound than that of his outward contiguity as an individual person."

Again it is necessary to realize that the work of the

Spirit is in the very nature of the case quiet and un-obtrusive. Otherwise it would be spoiled in its very operation. As Professor Olin A. Curtis put it: "The function of the Spirit is to carry on the work of Christ in the creation of a church or a new race, and this requires that there should be no intrusion upon human personality, but that the influence shall be such that men must listen. There can be no coercion, if the kingdom of God is to grow by the free turning of man to God, as the quiet, pervasive influence of his Spirit is felt in human life." He continues in these striking words: "It would be easy enough to make the whole race extremely religious by external coercive expe-dient. One crash of the planets would send every son of Adam to his knees." But there would be no ethical significance whatsoever in such a result. The work of the Spirit is very different from this. He is in the world to convince it of sin and to lead those who will listen into a new life of righteousness. Paul is in strict conformity with all that has been said concerning the identity of the work of the Spirit with the work of Christ when he declares that the fruits of the Spirit are "love, joy, peace, longsuffering, kind-ness, goodness, faithfulness, meekness, self-control" (Gal. 5. 22, 23).

Here again is another objective standard by which we may determine the genuineness of the work of the Holy Spirit in human life—it must always lead to righteousness of life and conduct. The human con-science is often spoken of as if it were a natural evolution which has paralleled the growth of mankind from his crude beginnings to his present stage of development. This has no meaning for anyone who knows what being led of the Spirit means. It is to him as personal as is his contact with his friends. It is not the working out of a natural law; it is the contact which finite men are privileged to have with the great infinite God himself. It is the voice of God speaking to the hearts of men. It may operate in all sorts of ways, but for one who has experienced what Christianity has in store for him, he may be sure that in all these ways God is seeking to convey to him the warnings and admonitions and impulses toward good which mankind testifies to wherever he has been led to think deeply of his moral and religious life.

And now, a little more closely, what is the Holy Spirit? Are we to speak of it as an influence only, affecting us as the memory of a great and good man? Some men are more appreciated after death than before—is this merely another case of posthumous influence? And are we to believe that the ideas and ideals of Jesus Christ live on and influence men the more as the years pass by? All these interpretations have been made, but the question which arises is, do they fit in with Jesus' words or the experience of Paul or Phillips Brooks or ourselves?

We may be very frank at this point and say that if they do, if these explanations are sufficient, there is little more to be said. The experience is real whatever the interpretation may be. We must, however, always remember that the doctrine of the Holy Spirit was not foisted upon the Christian Church by theologians. It did not come as a theory at all. It arose historically out of the experience of men and women in the Christian life, and only afterward did they attempt to theorize about it. They began to ask themselves what it all meant, and how it was to be related to other experiences. I do not believe it is possible for any other approach to be made to a satisfying doctrine of the Holy Spirit. It came out of experience and can only be interpreted by experience. It must arise afresh in experience, in the life of every Christian, if it is to exist at all. A man can never be convinced of the reality of the influence of the Holy Spirit unless he knows what it means as an actuality in his own life, and when once this experience has been his, he may theorize about it or he may not; it makes little difference to him, for he knows the reality. If he does theorize about it, it will be an attempt to put into a formulated statement the meaning of an experience which will forever reach deeper than it would be possible for him to frame in human language. When an experience such as this is warm and the heart throbbing with love for Christ and one is intent on doing his bidding, the tendency is to-day what it has always been, to find all other explanations inadequate, except that which makes the Holy Spirit a personal, immanent, invisible messenger of Jesus Christ to make possible the completion of his work in the world.

CHAPTER XIII

CAN I BELIEVE IN THE TRINITY AND STILL REMAIN A MONOTHEIST?

UNTIL comparatively few years ago the doctrine of the Trinity was considered the most important of all Christian doctrines, absolutely essential in the Christian structure. Missionaries even went so far as to require all candidates for Christian baptism to affirm their belief in this doctrine, which had been explained to them most carefully. We are told that the Moravian missionaries in the eighteenth century attempted to teach it to the depraved Hottentots in South Africa. They were finally brought to the very sane conclusion that it might be better not to attempt to teach this doctrine until the natives were able to count three! Surely, it was a wise decision to reach, a decision whose implications work out very much farther than its immediate application to the doctrine of the Trinity. Within recent years the situation has greatly changed. Many doctrines have been made the subject of controversy, but for one reason or another the Trinity is not among them. It may be because the doctrine is so difficult to state, or it may seem so far away from the actual life of a simple Christian believer. At any rate, it is left by itself alone, and many who do not actually scoff at it are willing not to raise the question of its truth. They feel that it is far too difficult or too abstract to be made the subject of discussion, especially when they desire to deal with those doctrines which have to do with human life at its ordinary levels. There is a tendency toward the simplification of our faith, and, in order to simplify, one of the doctrines which it is felt must not be emphasized is the doctrine of the Trinity.

I would state my own conviction at the very beginning of this discussion that there is a great difference between those truths which must be accepted in order to be a Christian at all and those beliefs which are only implied in other fundamental Christian doctrines. One of the dangers has always been that certain doctrines have been insisted on which have little or no relation to the everyday life of a simple Christian believer. Surely, it is not wise to insist on the acceptance of such teachings by the young man or woman seeking entrance to the Christian Church as truths necessary to salvation. But, on the other hand, we need to be careful that in the attempt to simplify and modernize the faith we do not "throw out the baby with the bath," as the Germans say. No doctrine can be thrust away summarily as useless which has almost since the beginning been proclaimed as an essential doctrine of the Christian Church—not without at least the most careful investigation. It may prove after we have made this investigation that there is more in the doctrine than we have supposed, and that, being presented in a different manner, it may answer certain questions which otherwise would be a source of trouble in the minds of thinking Christian people.

Let me say that my own interest in the doctrine of the Trinity has been very greatly increased by the study of other religions. I think it is true to say that every great religion has been compelled to deal with the doctrine of God, and when it does so it discovers that the problem is far from simple. There appears to be a kind of manifoldness implied which they had not suspected when they began to think about it. Hinduism has its Trimurti; Buddhism in its Mahayana form has found itself compelled to deal with an organization of divine beings, which suggests a fullness which was unknown in an earlier day. When the approach is made to Deity on the part of penetrating thinkers, there is something in absolute solitariness which is as likely to repel as to win the assent of the human mind. Even Mohammedanism, with its declaration of one God who will brook no "partners," seems uneasy and anxious lest some taint of the Trinitarian viewpoint should attach itself to its doctrines. In later years we have at least one Mohammedan writer who openly declares that the doctrine of a solitary God is an impossibility for the human mind. In other words, in one way or another the great religions find themselves confronted with an idea of God in some other than a simple, solitary form. They differ very greatly from what Christians have meant by the Trinity, but it is at least suggestive and significant, and that is all the value the present writer wishes to attach to their statements.

I must confess that I have little interest in the philosophical approach to the question. It is very interesting to study Hegel's claim that the dialectic, or movement of thought, which he discovered in the universe, must include Thesis, Antithesis, and Synthesis, and that this dialectic when applied to the Godhead makes necessary a threefold form of the divine nature. This is interesting, but it fails to be compelling. Why must God be as Hegel claims he is? Stronger reasons must be given than that God must fit in with a scheme which is of doubtful validity even when applied to earthly affairs.

. As has been the claim so frequently in these studies, here again the approach must be from the sure starting point of history. What can we learn from the New Testament? Consider two verses: "Go ye therefore, and make disciples of all the nations, baptizing them into the Name of the Father and of the Son and of the Holy Spirit" (Matt. 28. 19), and, "The grace of the Lord Jesus Christ, and the love of God, and the communion of the Holy Spirit, be with you alway" (2 Cor. 13. 14). Whatever else may be said of these passages, one thing is altogether evident, that Jesus Christ and his Spirit were so looked upon by the early Christians that they in the most natural manner placed them in the same category with God the Father.

The claim is by no means made that any formulated doctrine of the Trinity is to be found in the New Testament. It were well at the very beginning to let it be known that we can find no such thing until after the New Testament period. What we have in the New Testament is an experience and an attitude which grew out of the experience. The only possible result, when men began to think about their experience, was a doctrine which would put into tangible form that which previously had been only an experience and an attitude. We realize, of course, that this is what a true Christian doctrine is. It is not something pulled down out of the nebulous somewhere, but a statement made to express, as well as such a thing is possible, the intellectual implications of an experience which is real and vital. It is to justify to the intellect what the heart has experienced and what it demands. And when finally the doctrine was constructed, what did it say? It declared that the effect of Jesus Christ upon Christians was such that the only adequate thing they could do was to say that their idea of God must include Jesus Christ. The doctrine of the Spirit did not lag far behind. The book of Acts indicates very clearly that these early disciples lived under the guidance of the Spirit and could not but feel that it was God himself who was guiding them from day to day. So we have Father, Son, and Holy Spirit. These three were so intimately related and the disciples had such vital contacts with them that it was impossible to make any essential distinction. They all meant God to the early church. What they intended to say was that there could be no God at all without Father, Son, and Holy Spirit, a Trinity, or, better, a Tri-unity, three-in-one. And this is expressed in all the creeds and in our hymns and in countless "Trinity Churches" all over the world. What shall we do with it to-day? Is it an incumbrance or a true light to an intelligent understanding of what Christianity is at its very center?

Suppose for the moment we push the doctrine of the Trinity aside—what then? We may still believe in the one God of all, the Creator and Sustainer of the universe, and what more do we want? I must confess that I want several things not provided for in this attempted simplification. What would puzzle me most would be to know what had become of Jesus Christ. Men trusted him and came to look upon him as having the characteristics which they could only think of as godlike while he was with them, and they believed he was the living Christ, living still even though he had been taken away. What has become of him? Are we to find that one who had taken on a kind of final value while he was here has ceased to be of any particular significance now that he has passed on to the other side? If we speak of him as Master and Saviour and Lord and look upon him as the living Christ, what position does he occupy? Is he divine? Is he a man only? Or is he a semidivine being, halfway between man and God? We could scarcely apply to him the sacred names which we use if he were anything other than divine in the fullest sense. It would seem a little strange that the one who in his own life among men made God appear more wonderful than he had appeared even to the Old Testament prophets—that such a one should fall to an inferior place. If he has any significance at all in the Christian life of to-day beyond that of the memory of a good man who has died and whose influence is still felt, is it possible to assign to him any position less than that of being at the right-hand of God himself? The only way my sense of the fitness of things can be satisfied is to put Jesus Christ, the living One, there with the Father and the Spirit as together constituting all I mean by God.

One can already hear a chorus of objection to such statements. You have ceased to believe in one God and have given yourself to tri-theism; you have three Gods instead of one; you have given yourself to a speculation which has only made matters far worse than they were before. We cannot believe in any such God—that is, in a world where unity has become an absolute necessity at the center of things.

But I am not satisfied, and, if possible, I am about to make matters worse. There is another demand which I feel is not satisfied by the conception of a stark, solitary God, alone in his sublime majesty. I

must have a God who is the God of love, and you
have traveled a long distance on the way to make
such a conception very difficult, if not impossible, by
not being willing to place Jesus Christ with God at
the center of the universe. You will remember that
love is not one of the attributes of God in the Mohammedan religion. He is the lonely, solitary God in
Islam, and it would mean condescension for him to
give himself in love to those who do not share his
nature, but are merely his creatures, men and women
like ourselves. It would be very unwise to carry this
analogy very far, for the whole conception of God
and man is different in Mohammedanism as compared
with Christianity. But the question does come before
thinking men and asks for settlement. We have declared that love is of the very essence of the Divine
Being, and love must have an object or cease to be
love in the only sense we can think of with Jesus
Christ as our standard of what love is. If we must
provide a created world as the necessary object of
his love, we make God dependent upon his creation,
and this most Christians do not desire to do. There
are those who would claim that creation is an eternal
process and that we cannot think of God as anything
else than as an eternal Creator. But even if this were
so, there would at least be a logical dependence if not
a temporal one. God would still be compelled to be
the Creator of a universe in order to have an object of
love. This is speculation, to be sure, but even when
we are thinking in such a high realm we must still
think coherently. In the attempt to do so all the
individual thinker can do is to decide which idea
helps him most. He issues, then, no dogmatic statement; he merely testifies that when he thinks on such

themes one conclusion is more satisfying than another, and this is all that is claimed at this point.

Undoubtedly this is speculation and should never be put into our creeds as essential for the salvation of any man or woman. There are and have been thousands upon thousands of humble, simple, devoted men and women who have gone as far as it is possible for men and women to go in their devotion to God, who never knew much, if anything, concerning this doctrine. If it was not necessary for their salvation, neither is it necessary for ours. In fact, there are many wise men who have differed in their statements of this doctrine, so that if correctness of statement were necessary, many would be in a hopeless condition because of the inadequate manner in which in the estimation of others they have developed what is held to be essential to the faith.

Why, then, should we delve into the depths of speculation at all? Simply because we cannot help it. For anyone who is not only a Christian, but who desires to relate his Christianity with everything in the world and out of it, the time comes when it is necessary for him to try to think through the furthest implications of his faith and to reach conclusions if possible. When once this attempt is made the position of Jesus Christ in relation to God, not only when he was with his disciples in Galilee, but for us who desire to-day to commune with the invisible God, must be faced if we are to look squarely into all that is implied in the Christian religion. For those who have been able to reach the Trinitarian conclusion there come deep satisfactions which could scarcely be provided in any other way. Somehow Jesus appears in his right proportions and there is given to us a view of the meaning of God in the fullness of his being and nature which otherwise could not be reached at all.

The one great danger in speculations on this subject is that the doctrine may be so overstated that we find ourselves standing for three Gods instead of one. Let us remember, however, that all the great Christian utterances at this point have been very clear. There is but one God—there has been no hesitancy at this point. When we speak of three-in-one what is meant is that there is such a unity that their relation to us and to the world is as if there were but one center with which we have contact. There is but one purpose and will. It is the will of God, his one will for the world and men, that we find when we give ourselves to him.

It is very presumptuous, we are told, to declare we know so much about the inner processes of the Divine Being, which in the nature of the case are beyond our understanding. Are we not overbold when we declare that our God is not a lonely, solitary God, but that he is the triune God, completely unified in each act and attitude toward the children of men? This is the argument which is used by those who refuse to admit that we are able to make any affirmation concerning the inner life of the Godhead, except that he is the one all-knowing and all-powerful God by whom everything has been created and everything in the universe is sustained to-day. The question may be asked, on the other hand, whether the denial of the Trinity is not assuming to know almost as much about the inner being of God as the more positive declaration that God is three-in-one. If we do not know enough about the being of God to declare that he is three-in-one, do we know enough about it to declare that a Trinity is an impossibility? It would seem that one statement is about as presumptuous as the other. Shall we, then, declare ourselves to be utterly agnostic, or is there some more tangible way out of our difficulty?

Again we fall back on history. We do not know any more about the inner structure of the divine nature than we can discover in God's revelation of himself in Jesus Christ. What do we find when we examine this revelation? We see God in Jesus Christ and in his Spirit in such fullness that it does not seem presumptuous on our part to believe that we see God so clearly in his revelation because he is actually present himself in the revelation. We also believe that God is telling us as plainly as possible that Jesus Christ and the Holy Spirit are really divine, acting and doing things in men and among men in as real a sense as if we were told that God was performing those acts himself.

There is, then, but one God, manifesting himself in these three ways. That much is clear. Shall we not declare, then, that there are three manifestations, but that they are manifestations only and that they have nothing to do with the inner life of God himself? In all probability this would be our conclusion were it not for Jesus Christ himself who to-day as in the days of his flesh "cannot be hidden." Where shall we place him? How is he to be related to God? If he ceases to be God for us, we are put to it because God cannot be greater in all that makes him what he is than in his manifestation in Jesus Christ. We believe we see in Christ what God is really like, because he is by nature and character in a position to make that kind of revelation. And that could be done only by one who in some fashion is fundamentally one with God himself. In the ancient creeds the Father, the Son, and the Holy Spirit are called "Persons." It was their attempt to make clear what the triune nature of God was like. We admit to-day that this is exceedingly unsatisfactory. If the word "Person" when applied to God means the same that it does when we speak of human beings as persons, it is at once evident that it is altogether inadequate. Human personality connotes separateness and distinctness, so that it would be impossible for us to conceive of any three human beings so closely united to each other that we could speak of them in any real sense as three-in-one. They remain separate and distinct individuals with no inherent necessity of being one in all their attitudes and deeds, as is essential to the Christian conception of God. All we can say is that we do not know the inner processes of the divine life to the extent of being able to declare that we know how Jesus Christ can be so related to the Father and to the Spirit that these three could ever be one in the sense that we would speak of them as composing one God, the one center of creative energy in the universe. In the nature of the case the triune God can neither be pictured nor described. When we have experienced God as we see him in Christ, and realized the guidance of the Spirit, we are on the track of the deepest satisfaction, both intellectually and emotionally, when we declare that God is manifest to us in the Father and in the Son and in the Holy Spirit. We have seen and experienced God in Jesus Christ and in the working of the Spirit, and this has made God what he is for us. So, with all the difficulties involved, we deliberately make choice and affirm that the conception of God as Father, Son, and Holy Spirit, one God, triune but still one, does more for us than any alternative which has been proposed.

CHAPTER XIV

IS MAN THE MASTER OF HIS FATE?

"It matters not how strait the gate,
  How charged with punishments the scroll,
I am the master of my fate:
  I am the captain of my soul."[1]

THESE words of Ernest Henley, breathing defiance in the face of adverse fortune and illness, find a response in the breast of every man. But is it true? Is man really the master of his fate, the captain of his soul? This question implicitly or explicitly underlies about all of our thinking concerning the individual and his relationship to the universe. It simply will not down. Henry Sedgwick declared that it did not matter which way the question was answered; we were the same men anyway and acted in the same manner whatever we believed concerning the relation of a man to his own destiny. The conclusion he reached was that the whole discussion ought to be dropped; there was no profit in it; it made little or no difference in the way we acted. Professor George H. Palmer says that this reminds him of Aristotle's dictum, "If we must not philosophize, then we must philosophize." No matter what we do about it, we must deal with the question of human freedom, and it may turn out that much more hangs upon our attitude than Sedgwick and others would have us think.

---

[1] From *The Golden Treasury*. Reprinted by permission of The Macmillan Company, publishers.

It is impossible to make any advance in the consideration of this subject by saying that weak and unworthy men are on one side and the strong and noble on the other. It may be true that weak men have hidden behind a fatalistic doctrine, but we must also remember that some of the strongest men who have lived have done their work feeling that they were not free, but were determined by a force which they could not control. Of course, it is possible to discover unworthy results following the acceptance of a fatalistic creed, as among the followers of Mohammed, but we should never forget that John Calvin and Jonathan Edwards were determinists. They believed that what they did was predestined by the will of God; they were what they were because God willed it. There have been no greater heroes of the faith, men who have stood for political liberty and uprightness in private life as well as in public service, and yet they have felt that what they did was not the result of their own choice but was predetermined in the councils of God from the eternities.

We need to look a little more closely at the kind of determinism to which these men gave themselves. They felt that they were in the hands of an intelligent and loving God, a God who could be called Father and whose every purpose was to advance the good of men and to bring in a kingdom of righteousness on earth. This is a very different kind of determinism from that which we find to-day in the scientific world, a mechanistic and psychological determinism, which would assert that we as men are only a part of a great mechanism and that unalterable forces are acting upon us, causing us to do what we do and to be what we are. We cannot escape from their inevitable control. We may dream we are free, but it is only a dream. No matter what happens, we cannot be different. We are really helpless creatures bound fast in an enormous machine which keeps grinding through the ages without purpose or design and giving no evidence of being the result of the volition of an intelligent Creator or Director.

According to this theory we may be certain of many things—of everything if only we knew more. There can be no question that "given antecedents" are always followed by "invariable consequents." The only reason why we cannot predict human actions is that we are not able to discover all the antecedents. Were we able to penetrate into the past of any man's life and gather together all the factors which in any wise enter into his life now, it would be as easy to determine how that man would act under any given circumstance as it is for an astronomer to predict eclipses and to determine tides and other celestial and natural phenomena. We might then have prepared a kind of Nautical Almanac of human life to which we might go in order to discover how a man with such and such characteristics and background would act under such and such conditions. Of course no one now claims to be able to do any such thing, but it is only because we have not learned all the factors in the life of any individual. The theory holds good, even though its application to given situations may be delayed for years, if not for centuries to come.

A modification has been introduced into the theory in recent years. Our actions may be determined not only by circumstances, but by circumstances plus the individual character of the man. Determinists have been classified as "hard" and "soft," the hard determinists being those who lay emphasis on circumstance as the chief factor determining a man's life. The "soft" determinists are those who hold that a man's character determines the conduct of a man in addition to the circumstances and antecedents of his life. According to this modification, if only we knew a man through and through, all that has gone into his making, we could tell just what he would do at any point of decision. Now, while this is a real modification from external determinism, the fact remains that a man is not free. He is determined, if not by circumstance, by his character, and is so bound down that at any single point he really has no choice between two alternatives. There are no new departures, no surprises. A man simply must do what the momentum of his life up to that given point determines and everything else is utterly impossible.

Let us be very free to recognize that the freedom a man has, if there be any freedom at all, is a limited freedom. We can never get away from the fundamental fact that we live in a universe of law and that causation never ceases. There are "no gaps in nature"; "all space is occupied by causation." If we can find no cause for anything that takes place, it is not because it does not exist, but merely because we have not been able to find it. Scientific study is to a considerable extent motivated by the desire to find causes, causal explanation being explanation in the world of science. When we can tell how anything became what it is, then we have settled one of the most important problems which faces anyone who studies the world in which we live. There is nothing which escapes the application of this law of causation. The human mind also is subject to law, and these laws are being brought to light very rapidly at the present time in the careful study which is being made of the human mind and its processes in our physiological, biological, and psychological laboratories. The confusion in which psychology now finds itself is caused by the fact that so much new light has come within recent years that the more constructive work of relating all the facts, not only one to another, but to all other knowledge in the universe, has not advanced so as to keep pace with the sheer accession of knowledge. When we shall have been able to digest much more completely all that has been done in the last fifty years we may begin to have a science of psychology, but it is still only in promise and not in fulfillment.

We must also realize that we cannot prove the fact of human freedom. The reason lies immediately at hand. Freedom is an inner conviction in our minds which cannot be measured by any instruments of precision. It cannot be observed from the outside; it is purely a subjective fact. We have an immediate experience of freedom and that is about all there is to it. We feel we can do one thing rather than the other. In the moral realm we feel we ought to do one thing and not another. All this would lose point if an open possibility did not lie before us. And yet with the tremendous strength of this conviction we can only testify to its presence and cannot prove (using proof in the strict sense of demonstration) it is anything else but a feeling on our part.

We must see, however, how deeply implanted this feeling is in the whole human race. There is no wonder that it has become a deeply ingrained conviction which it is next to impossible to eradicate. How is it

CHAPTER XV

WHY DO WE NEED FORGIVENESS?

Why do we need forgiveness? The answer can only be because we have sinned and are sinners. So what we have before us is a consideration of the fact, the meaning, and the significance of sin. Why, then, should the discussion have been given the title it has and not something about sin itself? Simply because it was from the standpoint of the effect of sin on our relationship with God that the whole subject took hold of the mind of the writer and this stating of the question put the subject in the clearest manner for him. Sin, then, from this standpoint is that which makes forgiveness necessary. So we have two questions, What is sin? and What is forgiveness?

One of the most important elements in the study of sin is to realize that sin is not something which can be separated from the sinner. In the religion of the more primitive peoples and that of many who have advanced a considerable distance away from early forms, sin is often looked upon as a man might look upon his clothes, something which he wears but which can be taken off and laid aside as if not connected vitally with his life and person. He can get rid of them and put them far away. There are many statements in the Bible which would indicate that the writers had this conception in mind. In a very beautiful passage we are told that

"As far as the east from the west,
  So far hath he removed our transgressions from us."

In the book of Leviticus, sixteenth chapter, is the law concerning the scapegoat. Once a year the high priest was to confess the sins of the people, and then in a real sense take these sins in his hands, place them on the head of the scapegoat, and drive the goat far out in the wilderness bearing away the sins of the people. In a very real sense the sins were conveyed to the goat. But if we go further in the course of revelation and come into the New Testament, sin is looked upon as a far more personal matter, something which adheres to and is a part of the man himself. And now with the coming of the psychological attitude it becomes apparent that sin can be nothing else than a certain attitude of mind, an act of the will, a direction taken by a person. As true a statement as can be made is that sin is a sinner sinning. It is his personal attitude, it is the sinner doing this or failing to do that. When this conception is well fixed in the mind the whole question of forgiveness changes form; it becomes a far more personal matter than when forgiveness was looked upon as the removal of something which could be separated from the sinner like his watch or fountain pen.

I suppose we will all agree that sin is a fact in human experience and history. Not only is this recognized in the Bible but in the sacred books of other religions. Every court of law is a recognition of the fact that men have an ideal of rectitude to which they are expected to conform by the community. It is one of the major themes in all great literature, and some of the most striking statements that can be found of sin and its awful effects are in the dramatic and epic literature of the ages. It comes out in the modern novel as well. When we come home to our own experience

it is there always staring us in the face and warping
if not destroying what might otherwise be beautiful
and noble and pure and good. Whence did so dreadful a blight come into human life? The explanation
which has been offered through the course of Christian
history is that sin came into the world as the result of
the sin of the first man Adam and his wife Eve in the
garden of Eden. Does this explain it all? Another
set of facts must be interpreted now that we have
information concerning the development of man in the
long course of the evolution of animate nature. It has
become necessary to listen to God when he speaks
through nature and history and conscience, as well as
in the Bible and in Jesus Christ. What we hear when
we allow ourselves to be led back into the very beginnings of human life is that man had a long animal
ancestry and that he has inherited from this ancestry
his animal nature. I do not know how it is possible
to deny this fact, but we must remember that it is
only a part of the complete fact which makes man
what he is. He is an animal, but very much more
than an animal. He possesses self-consciousness and
self-determination, and neither of these is possessed
even by the highest animals. He is a person as they
are not, and this makes all the difference in the world.
It separates him by a very deep chasm from the animal
creation. Nature has no way for accounting for this
difference. What we find is that man has a moral
nature which the animals do not have, and because
he has a moral nature sin is possible. From the first
he possessed the power of choice and could feel regret
and a sense of guilt. The sad fact is that he did actually sin, and all succeeding generations have done
likewise. It is not sin in the animals to be as they

are. It is not sin in man to have an animal nature
which in so many respects binds him to the natural
world. The possibility of sin arises when the instincts which he possesses in common with the animals
are subject to direction in his case. An animal never
goes wrong, for he has no possibility of choice. A man
can go wrong because in the use of his instincts he
may choose to abuse his opportunities. Let us be
thankful that he may also use them in a wise way
which will lead to strength and character. Along with
the possibilities of misuse is the possibility of noble
and helpful use, and this brings the joy which man
may have but which animals know nothing about.

There have been those who have been pleased to
picture the antithesis of man before "the fall" of
Adam and since. Before he fell Adam is pictured as a
paragon of excellence and intelligence, who afterward
was reduced to so low an estate that he transmitted
to his children a nature which some have gone to the
extent of declaring is "totally depraved." The contrast is all too glaring. Sin always injures, but one
can scarcely feel as he looks out on the world to-day
that in one fell swoop man was hurled from being a
Plato down to the level of a moron or a sneak thief.
The story as it is told with such vividness in the third
chapter of Genesis is psychologically true. It is a
wonderful picture of the process of temptation and of
sinning. But it is very hard, in view of all the other
facts, to believe that man's whole subsequent state,
unfortunate as it is, was his solely because the first
man sinned in the manner that is described in the
third chapter of Genesis. One of the incontrovertible
facts is that death had been in the world a long time
before man emerged as a man. Death undoubtedly

took on a new significance after man had sinned, but it is scarcely possible to say that sin is accountable for death, as if death would never have occurred had it not been for the sin of man.

What influence did the sin of early man have on his descendants?—on us, to bring it straight home? Did we share in it as many of the older theologians said? "When Adam sinned," can we say, "we all jined in"? Did we share in this sin either realistically or representatively, so that we can justifiably be punished for it even though we may not have sinned ourselves? Was our nature totally depraved by that one sin, as many of the older theories would intimate? I am sure I do not desire to minimize the dreadful results of sin, but I am quite sure it is as easy to exaggerate sin as it is to minimize its influence. How many have called themselves "worms of the dust," thinking thus to place themselves in the right attitude in God's universe. Sin can bring a man very low, but the attitude which Jesus always had toward sinning men and women was never that of dealing with a creature as if it were as low as a worm. He always seemed to see in everyone a child of God in whom there were possibilities of development which went beyond anything which the person himself had ever dreamed of. When men and women come up as remarkably and even as quickly as they do out of the depths of degradation at the touch of the gospel it is good evidence that they were not utterly depraved, but that the gospel found something on which it could work. The race has suffered dreadfully because of sin, but not in the sense that man lost everything when Adam first sinned. Hereditary taint is still a dark subject which we do not completely understand, but it does not determine everything a man does. Other factors enter in which are equally important. Each man as he comes to the age of accountability, simply because he is a man, has his own personal decisions to make, and here is the opening for sin, and for nobility too.

If sin, then, is a fact, let us look a little more closely at it. It is not negligible; it is an awful fact in human experience, a very positive and blameworthy thing. It is not "good in the making"; it tears down all good. It is not an amiable or unfortunate weakness to be passed by with mere regret, but a responsible attitude or act, which might have been different and which brings guilt and a sense of shame into the human breast. Accordingly, sin is self-will as contrasted with the acceptance of the will of God. It is selfishness as contrasted with neighborliness and helpfulness. It is presumption as contrasted with consideration of the rights of others. And, finally, sin is alienation, separation from the one wronged. It is the breaking of a relationship of love, cooperation, and service with God. It is a disruption in ideals and principles. It is separation from the love and goodness of the great, loving God. It is a very personal thing, in the last analysis a matter of relationship between persons. Sin separates one from the one sinned against and finally from God, the source of life and good.

This brings us to the question which was suggested by the title of this study. What is forgiveness? It is that which overcomes the effect of sin, and since the essence of sin is that it separates from God, forgiveness is the restoration of that broken relationship. It is a relationship which has been broken because man in his sin separated himself from all that was good, including God himself. I wish it might be possible to make this so clear that it would affect all thinking about our relation to God. The tendency has often been to look upon forgiveness as a judicial affair, the declaration of a judge that the prisoner at the bar has been pardoned and will now escape the punishment which otherwise might have been his fate. Whenever we see forgiveness from the standpoint of Jesus, who called God Father, the whole subject is very deeply changed. Forgiveness is not essentially a declaration at all. It is an act in which the injured party receives the one who is forgiven back into the old relationship of confidence and intimacy. There can be no forgiveness where this restoration does not take place; otherwise it is merely a matter of the lips and not real forgiveness at all. It reminds one of the story of a man who was about to die and who had an acquaintance against whom he had a grudge. Not wishing to die with this grudge in his heart, he sent for his acquaintance and said to him: "If I dies, I forgives thee all. But if I lives, the old grudge hangs good." There was no forgiveness here at all, only the attempt on the part of a man who knew he should not cherish a grudge in his heart to try in his own eyes to appear better as he passed over into the great beyond. Real forgiveness may have nothing to say with the lips, but when the repentant sinner comes back and there is real forgiveness, the old relationship is restored. The forgiveness lies in that restoration itself.

There is no more beautiful illustration of this than in the most beautiful of all Jesus' parables, the parable which we speak of as the prodigal son. Nothing is said about forgiveness in this parable, but the thing itself is there. The father was on the lookout for the boy, and when he came, went out to meet him and immediately restored him to the old place of love and confidence in his heart. This was forgiveness and needed no words to declare that the forgiveness had been accomplished—the restoration of the old relationship was the forgiveness itself.

It is well to know that real forgiveness is a matter in which both sides must have a part. A man may have the forgiving heart and eagerly desire to restore the other to the former confidence, but such a restoration is utterly impossible until the one who has done wrong has experienced such a sense of wrongdoing and the need of a changed heart, that he comes back to the injured party wholly changed, penitent and humbled and eager for a new life. Then, and then only, is the complete act of forgiveness possible, for then the two hearts may again beat as one, and this, again, is the essence of forgiveness. There is nothing more wonderful in human life than real forgiveness. There is a great deal which travels under the name of forgiveness which is merely a matter of the lips or smacks of courts of law. But genuine forgiveness, which means an inward change which makes possible a renewed life on the old basis of trust and confidence —when this actually occurs, the veil has been rent apart and we catch a view of the divine in human life as clearly as in any experience possible to man. Here is where love can play its largest part, overcoming the hatred, the resentment, and the hurt which one feels because of an injury, and so enlarging the heart that there is not only the willingness but an eager desire that the one who has done the injury may be so changed in heart that a complete restoration may be accomplished, a reconciliation which will make possible again fellowship on the old basis. In fact, the fellowship may even be deeper because of the love which has come into the injured heart and because the sense of gratitude which that love has awakened in the one who has done wrong has deepened the relationship and made possible the expression of confidence and love which may never have been known before. It is the miracle of human relationships; it is where human nature rises nearest to the divine.

When we are led to think of sin thus as a personal matter we become more careful in the use of terms. Are the sins which a man commits forgiven or is he himself forgiven? The answer must come very quickly that it is he himself who is forgiven, for sin is himself acting thus or in having this attitude or that. Consequently, it is not the canceling of a debt, nor is it the separation of a man from something which can be cast away as a soiled garment, but is a new relationship made possible by his sincere repentance. He must be forgiven by the power of love and is received back by God a changed man. He is the same man so far as his personality is concerned, but changed because the old attitude has been left behind. He is now full of gratitude and love and the desire for fellowship and communion with his Father. He has become a new creature, utterly different from his old self.

CHAPTER XVI

WHAT MUST I DO TO BE SAVED?

WE call to mind the simple and direct reply made by Paul to this question when it was asked by the Philippian jailer, "Believe on the Lord Jesus Christ, and thou shalt be saved." This might seem to be all the answer needed, were it not for the fact that many things are implied in this answer which have a significance which we must see. The whole subject is so related to life and to other doctrines that it is necessary to look at the subject broadly, if we are to understand the meaning of the answer which has just been given.

But before asking what we must do in order to be saved, it may be well to find out what salvation itself means in Christianity. We use the word "salvation" very frequently, but it is doubtful if we realize its real significance. Since it is so important we ought to be very sure what we mean when we say that we are saved. One of the answers which is frequently made to the question is that being saved means to be safe, especially in the time to come after death. Then, if we are saved, we shall surely go to heaven and escape hell. This is put quite bluntly, but it represents in as few words as possible the actual situation in the minds of thousands and thousands of Christian people.

I am quite sure that being saved includes just what has been stated—a man who is saved will surely go to heaven. In a later study we shall try to understand a little better what going to heaven means, but whatever of joy and of wonder and of satisfaction there is in that experience must be included in salvation according to Christianity. But when this has been said we have not yet touched the most important aspect of the answer to our question. Just as it stands, to say that being saved means that we shall go to heaven after we die is to have an essentially selfish conception of its meaning. It may be a very refined kind of selfishness. It may be a selfishness devoid of crudity, devoid of gross elements, in which the pleasures toward which we look forward are of the finest kind, yet nevertheless it is a selfish attitude at best. We may put it in another way by saying that everything in this answer is centered in oneself, it is an appeal to self-interest, it is a desire for rewards and a very earnest expectation of pleasure as contrasted with the punishment of hell. We want to be safe, we want to escape something we do not like. Is this the best we have to offer? Let us be very clear at this point. If it is, we have not risen in principle above Mohammedanism, nor have we reached a level as high as the best in Hinduism or Buddhism, not to speak of other faiths.

The Mohammedan idea of heaven is gross, and every pure-minded Christian must turn away from it with very deep moral aversion. The heaven or heavens in Hinduism or Buddhism hold out very little which could commend itself to one who has been brought up on the Bible and its idea of the future life. The particular things which fill the mind of those who look forward to paradise in these other religions are on a lower level than the experience to which Christians look forward as they realize the meaning of the immortality depicted in our Scriptures. But with all that has been said, we must realize that that is not the point. Whether the paradise be on a high level or on a low level, whether the experiences are ennobling or degrading, if our conception of salvation is that we are to inherit a reward, and that reward is what fills our minds, it is all on the level of selfishness. The best minds of Hinduism and Buddhism turn away and declare that men should not be looking out for personal gain and rewards as they peer out into the future. If our salvation is of this character it is like the little girl who said that she liked one man better than another because one gave her candy and the other did not. This, of course, is on a very much lower plane, but the principle is the same. In adolescence again it is the boy who says he would rather be with one man than another because one takes him in his automobile and the other has no automobile in which he can ride. And now, lifting it up into adult life, into the realm of religion, we may put the same thing in this fashion, that we are going to be children of God and obey his commands and love Christ because by so doing we are sure to reach heaven thereby. The object in each case is quite different, but, again let it be repeated, we do what we do for the sake of the rewards that come to us. That is our ultimate ground for accepting Christ and receiving his salvation—if this view commands our allegiance.

But this is not the distinctive Christian appeal at all. If we want to put the matter in a truly Christian way, so as to show it in its essential difference from what has just been presented, it might be stated in this form, that salvation means to be saved from one's sins so that he may become like Jesus Christ and be pleasing to him. Saved to be like Jesus may be the shortest way in which to state the essential fact in Christian salvation. When it is stated thus there is no appeal even to enlightened selfishness or self-interest. It is all transformed by the idea that to be saved is to be like Christ.

Let us realize how deeply this cuts into our whole idea of the meaning of Christianity. The present writer can remember the day when he spoke before audiences and told them that the first word which Christianity speaks to a man is "Come, get something for yourself; be saved." And after that is accomplished there is another word which Christianity has to speak: "Go, serve Christ, help bring in the kingdom of God, be truly unselfish in your life." I have been led to believe that this division of the call of Christianity into two separate appeals is entirely unnecessary. Is it not true in our church life to-day that we feel it is necessary to be "saved," but more or less optional to serve? Do we not hold that when a man believes in Christ he is "saved," but that sacrifice and service are connected with his salvation only superficially, not vitally? This surely is all wrong. Whenever salvation is seen to be salvation from our sins, salvation to be like Jesus, we realize that service is just as much of the essence of salvation as is any personal benefit which we may look upon as being connected with our experience. It is the call to character, character as we see it in Jesus Christ, and when we look at Jesus, what do we find? It was a character in which goodness overflowed, in which purity and honor and nobility characterized all that he did and said, but at the same time, without any possibility of discovering a cleavage between the two, it was a charcater whose other feature, without which it could not be what it was, was service. So that being saved in Christianity is to be saved from our sins in order that we may become Christlike, and to be Christlike means to develop a character like his and to become a servant of humanity as he was. It is not, then, primarily to lift up heaven as a desirable place to spend eternity, nor to paint hell in lurid colors as a place to avoid. It is a life to be lived here, and now, of such quality that the touch of eternity is already on it.

This conception makes the task of salvation far more significant and more difficult than otherwise it might be. So frequently when salvation is mentioned it is looked upon as salvation from the consequences of our sins, instead of a salvation from sinning, from the very sins themselves. Our memories in America quite easily bring back the picture of a certain great lawyer who a few years ago defended two wealthy, intelligent young men who had very brutally murdered a little boy. This lawyer set himself to save these men from the gallows and succeeded in doing so. His defense resulted in saving these men from the consequence of their evil deeds insofar as that is under the control of the state. But what if this lawyer had had in mind to save these young men from their sins, from their evil natures, from their utter selfishness? It is quickly evident that his task would have been superhuman, that what he had to do was comparatively easy in contrast with this task of attempting to save men from their dispositions, from their nature, the nature out of which their evil act came. So in Christianity we have a salvation from the consequences of a man's sins. There can be no doubt about that. But this is relatively a slight task, a very little part of what God has in mind when he seeks to save men. What he desires is that men shall be transformed, made over again, so that they shall no longer desire to do the things they did, so that new purposes will be formed in their minds and hearts and they shall become unselfish and loving to all men. This is the task of Christian salvation, and when we look at it from this standpoint it causes it to seem a far more wonderful thing than when we look at it in any other light.

This will undoubtedly help us to put new meaning into a phrase frequently heard, "Preaching Christ." What does it imply to preach Christ? Surely it must include preaching him as the world's Saviour, who died for man and thereby breaks the hardened human heart. But assuredly it is more than this. It means preaching him as he is in the Gospels, tracing his life as he talked to the people who gathered round him in Galilee and Jerusalem, as he gave Himself in unselfish service to afflicted men and women, as he sorrowed over their sins, as he showed himself happy in the company of little children, and as he journeyed with his disciples, leading them off to the mountainside, where he might have opportunity for rest and time to instruct them in the message which they were to proclaim. The purpose which anyone should have in mind in proclaiming Jesus is to make him so attractive in all the features of his life that men will want to be like him. This has its negative side also, a sincere turning away from the evil life that has been lived. In other words, to be saved is a matter of character interpreted in terms of Jesus Christ. I do not want to be misunderstood at this point. I have never felt nor do I feel now, that salvation is *by* character, but I am quite sure that it is salvation *to* character. We are saved by Christ and not by ourselves, nor by our own characters, but we are saved by Christ to become like himself, and this means acquiring a Christlike character.

And now having looked at this question of salvation and having tried to see it in the light of Jesus Christ, we may come to the main question of this study, what must I do to be saved?—to be saved in the sense in which we have just defined the term. Every religion has its answer to this question. By some salvation is secured by buying off a malevolent Deity, by others propitiating the Deity by sacrifice, by others through mental intuition or rising to a new and liberating thought, which in itself brings salvation. In other faiths salvation comes by sacramental magic and in still others it may come by the suppression of desire or obedience to a code of laws or by correct living or by self-inflicted tortures. Many are the methods, only a few of which have been mentioned in this list, by which men hope to achieve the kind of salvation which their religion holds out. The answer which we must give to the question is determined partially at any rate by the kind of salvation Christianity holds out, and this we have tried to describe in the previous pages. What is it we are after when we desire to be saved? We are after a new life, a new character in which we shall be saved from our sins and look forward to close fellowship with God beginning here and extending down through the eternities. What are we to do in order that this may be accomplished? Let us again look at Paul's answer to the Philippian jailer, "Believe on the Lord Jesus Christ, and thou shalt be saved." What does "belief" in this answer mean?

Is it a purely intellectual thing, an acceptance of the fact that Jesus Christ is our Saviour as we find it stated in the Bible? Undoubtedly there is an intellectual element. We would be hopeless without it. The only question is, Has not too exclusive an emphasis been placed upon this side of the process? We must realize that all through Paul's writings the word "faith" means something deeper than intellectual apprehension. It might be expressed better by the word "trust," taking Jesus for what he says he is and then resting upon him for all that he can do for us. I think it is necessary to look even a little more closely at its meaning. Does there not lie back of the Christian idea of salvation the fundamental thought that every really significant change which takes place in human character is brought about by personal contacts? It is undoubtedly true among men. Is it different in our relation with God? Is not God the only one who can save and are we not to be saved by coming into contact with him? Are we not saved by receiving his nature? Are we not to receive the character we desire by the inflow into our poverty-stricken lives of the fullness of God? But what part does Jesus play? In the next study we shall consider the significance of God's initiative and the sacrifice he made in Christ Jesus. We may anticipate here, however, and state that it was Jesus who showed us the heart of God, that it was Jesus who manifested what godlikeness was, that it was Jesus who opened the way to God, that it was Jesus through whom the life of God comes to the lives of men, and that it was Jesus who is the light in our darkness, showing the way out. And when we believe on Jesus Christ what really happens is that we come to him in trust, be-

lieving that in him we come in contact with the Great
Father. When we are related to Christ in this personal way we are really in touch with Him from whom
all good flows and with whom are the destinies of life,
even the eternal God himself. And it is through this
contact that salvation comes flowing into our lives,
making them over again.

Whenever the word "faith" is mentioned, we must
remember that there is an element of risk. If everything could be demonstrated, as that two and two
make four, there would be no element of faith. If we
could actually see God as we do the trees outside the
window, there would be no risk, but there is a venture
when we give ourselves to Christ. We risk all in believing that we are relating ourselves to Him who
brings us into the very presence of God. By contact
with him we venture to believe we have that relationship which is able to make character over and conform us to the image of Jesus Christ himself. It is
of the very essence of faith that it makes demands on
us which draw out the very best in human nature
and thus makes every element develop into maturity
and strength. Only in love and trust and confidence
can life find a center around which it can be organized.
This is true of our human friendships, how much more
when we come into the presence of God himself, who
is the center of all life! Does anything stand in the
way of this step which we may take? Again, as we
saw in the last study, there is just one fact and that is
the sin from which we need to be saved. We cannot
save ourselves from either the consequences of our
sins, or from the sins themselves, but God in his wisdom has willed that we cannot be saved by him unless
we fulfill certain conditions. These conditions are not

such as are found written in statute books. They are
the conditions which inhere in personal relationships.
No two persons can ever be friends when one has done
an injury to the other unless there be genuine repentance on the part of him who has done the wrong.
Neither can God save a man from his sins until, with
the vision of Christ before him, a man begins to loathe
his sinning and turns away from it and begins to
desire with his whole heart to be pure and upright as
Jesus was. When this has been done repentance has
taken place and God can do his part in order that a
man may be saved.

So, then, what we must do to be saved is to repent,
or turn away from our sins, and place our trust in
Jesus Christ that he will bring us into that personal
contact with God which brings every good thing to
pass in human life. But is this all? Surely, this man-
ward side is most important, but is it all? By no
means; in Christianity there is a sense in which man
seeks God, but Christianity is unique in that we discover in a profound sense that God is out seeking man.
There is a "divine initiative" which marks off Christianity from other faiths, and to this we must now
turn, and to strike at the very center of the whole
problem, we are next to ask, "What interest have we
in the death of Christ?"

CHAPTER XVII

WHAT INTEREST HAVE WE IN THE DEATH OF CHRIST?

How is it possible to compress into a single short study anything adequate on so important a theme? Again, as in other studies, all that can be attempted is to point out what seem to be the crucial issues and open the way toward conclusions which will grip the mind of those seeking light on this difficult, yet all-important, subject.

We may approach the question from the standpoint of Jesus' own words and deeds. In the episode at Cæsarea Philippi Jesus asked the disciples who they took him to be. Peter, ever the spokesman of the twelve, answered that he was the Christ, the Messiah of expectation. Jesus at once began to lead them into an appreciation of the meaning of the Messiahship as he saw it, and we have the startling words, "The Son of man must suffer many things . . . and be killed" (Mark 8. 27-33). There is a "must" here, some kind of necessity; but why must Jesus suffer and die in order to be in the true sense the Messiah? Jesus does not give an answer, but one thing is very clear, that in his mind the Messianic kingdom cannot come without suffering and death. But why was that necessary? I am led to feel that the necessity Jesus felt resting on him was an inner moral and spiritual necessity, not something which compelled him from the outside to suffer and die in order that he might fulfill the Messiahship. The principle of vicarious sacrifice is the deepest principle in human life; it is the most far-reaching principle in the universe. It speaks the universal language, that of unselfish love. If Jesus is to inaugurate a kingdom which should win men and win them completely, he must base it on the deepest foundation known in human experience. The Son of man must suffer and die because only in that way could he penetrate to the depths of the human heart and build a kingdom which could not be moved. Undoubtedly, there was more in the mind of Jesus than that, but this at least was there, and nothing can exaggerate its importance.

In the account we have of the Last Supper (Mark 14. 22–25) which Jesus ate with his disciples we find Jesus at the close of the meal performing a highly symbolical act. He took bread and a cup of wine and gave them to his disciples telling them to take the bread as his body and to drink the wine as his blood. He did not partake of them himself, he *gave* them to his disciples. It was symbolic of something he was about to do for them. He spoke of his blood as that of a new covenant with God into which men might enter because of the sacrifice he was making. Men might now come into a relationship with God which had something unique about it and which was possible only because of what Jesus was about to do. Again, we are not given an explanation of why this was necessary and how such a sacrifice could bring it about, but one does not need to read between the lines to see that there is something in the sacrifice of Jesus Christ which was so complete and so wonderful that a new era was being ushered in, a time when men could enter into relations with God impossible before.

Again, a few hours after eating the last meal with his disciples Jesus passed through an experience of deep agony in the Garden of Gethsemane (Mark 14. 26, 32–36). He prayed in deep distress that "the hour might pass away from him" and that "this cup" might be removed. Why was he so deeply moved? What did Jesus mean by "the hour" and "this cup"? On the very surface of the narrative they can have significance only in connection with the awful death which was so evidently just before him. Was it the pain, the ignominy, and disgrace of such a death which caused such agony even in anticipation? By what we may feel is an unerring instinct, the Christian Church has always been convinced that more than this kind of anticipation was present to account for all the factors in the situation. There was something wrong with mankind which was making heavy demands on Jesus and without which his agony was inexplicable. A number of explanations have been offered which we need not here set down. The one which has registered itself in the mind of many Christians as most helpful is that Jesus was entering into the realization of the awful horror of sin as only a spotless soul could. It swept over his spirit. He saw its meaning as God saw it. He was realizing "the sorrow of the Infinite Father over the wrongdoing of his human children." Could he bear its weight? He turned away in horror. It was the bitterest cup which had ever been pressed to the lips of a living being, yet it was what God had experienced since man first sinned. To die, as he saw he must if he were to usher in a new day in which man could enter into a new relationship with God—to die, and thus to enter into the meaning of sin as God saw it and to show men what that meaning was, how could he stand it? Could it not be removed? Was there no other way? Yet, yet if it were the way his Father had chosen, he would drink the cup to the dregs, and "God's greatest victory on earth was won." God could now do for man in his sin what otherwise he, even he, could not do. He could reveal himself completely. Sin meant what Jesus would show men it meant to God. But more than this, Jesus could show as it had never been shown what a God he was, that his heart was full of love, a love willing to suffer and suffer to the uttermost, that men might turn from their sin and be received back to the Father-heart of God.

We now come to the crucifixion itself (Mark 15. 21–39, 45). Jesus was put to death, he died, but we may go further and with justice say that there was such complete acquiescence in God's will that Jesus was not passive in the experience through which he passed. He *gave* up his life. There was something voluntary and creative about his death which lifts it in its significance above all the examples of supreme sacrifice the world has ever witnessed. And again the question arises, why? and how? And again the lips of Jesus are silent, so far as the answer to these questions is concerned. How we would appreciate at least a hint! How much writing, much of it to little profit, would have been saved! We would then have had a theory of the atonement to which one could point as final and authoritative. But before we have proceeded far along this line in our thinking we may realize that it is better as it is. The final fact in Christianity, the cross of Calvary, is not a word but a deed. It speaks a more universal language than any explanation could. Words fail to plumb the depths of human experience; the deed itself is inescapable and when seen penetrates as deeply as human experience itself. We may come with our explanations, but they are all incomplete and partial. It is better to challenge the human mind and heart to look at the figure of Jesus crucified, believing that the touch of the divine will be felt more deeply by the simple realization that Jesus died, that he gave himself up for me, than by explanations which can never go as far as is needed to break the heart of sinful man and turn it in grateful love to the Saviour of Mankind.

These are the thoughts suggested by study of the experience of Jesus. They do not offer what is worthy to be called a theory of the atonement, but they point toward it. They have the advantage of coming out of the gospel story as it stands instead of forcing that story into the Procrustean bed of a theory.

The question arises, Can we or ought we to proceed further? I do not believe it is possible to stop at this point, even though something important has been gained. The best proof of this statement is that the human mind has through the centuries made the bold attempt to peer deeper, even though the death of Christ must always remain a mystery in part at least. We must take the time to look at some of these attempts, though it be but for a moment.

It seems utterly incredible to-day that the mind of Christian people could entertain a theory of the atonement for well on to a thousand years which to us is contrary to so much which is true of our religion. According to this orthodox conception, man was in the hands of Satan because of sin. The death of Christ was the ransom price paid by God for his liberation. Satan accepted the offer thinking thereby to have Christ placed in his power. He did not know, however, that Christ was a Divine Being. So he was outwitted by God, Christ slipping through his grasp through the resurrection, and thus Satan was the loser all around. He had given man up by accepting Christ's death as the ransom price, and then lost Christ too because he could not be held fast by death. What a strange perversion, but it has one good point as contrasted with some later theories, that it kept God and Christ together, working in unison for the same object, the salvation of man.

The beginning of the end of such theorizing came when Anselm (1033–1099) attempted an explanation of the sacrifice of Christ on more reasonable lines. He held that the death of Christ satisfied the honor of God which had been injured by man's sin. His honor was vindicated by punishment, which was essential to such a vindication, and which the sinless Jesus bore voluntarily because of the love he had for men. When his honor had thus been vindicated, God granted to Christ the privilege of releasing from the penalty of their sins those who believed in him. The important word in the theory of Anselm, and in that of many from that time to our own who have followed his general direction in their thinking, is the word "satisfaction." God's honor or his justice had to be "satisfied." It could only be satisfied by the actual infliction of punishment. The only escape from merited punishment is made possible in that Jesus Christ took our place, became our "substitute," bore the penalty of our sins, and thus opened the way for our forgiveness. The question which thousands have asked and ask to-day when confronted with this theory is, Why must justice be vindicated in this way and in this way alone? Is

there no way in which God can forgive without the
merited punishment being actually inflicted on an
innocent being?

That there is a better way is the answer given
by those who are convinced that God's forgiveness
is free and that there is no hindrance to forgiveness
so far as the honor and justice of God are concerned.
The death of Christ was necessary for another reason.
There was danger, if God's forgiveness should become
operative without penalty, that the divine government
of the world might be upset or at least dislocated or
endangered. This would take place if men should
conclude that sin was not so terrible a fact after all
and that no great injury would follow in the train of
wrongdoing. In order to make this forever impossible Jesus died the awful death on Calvary to im-
press men with the character of sin and its disruptive
effect in the universe. This theory, which is asso-
ciated with the name of Grotius (1583-1645), the
Dutch theologian and jurist, is called the "govern-
mental theory," its deep concern being that the moral
government of the world should not suffer in the
relation God was willing to sustain to men.

In contrast to both these historic theories there is
another which has had a long history and which has
commended itself to the minds of many in recent
years. It is called the "moral influence" theory, according to which the death of Christ was needed,
neither as a satisfaction of God's justice nor as a
means to insure that God's government of the universe should remain intact, but in order to show
men how deep God's love was and thus break the
hearts of men by a realization of that fact. This
theory was first formulated by Abelard (1079-1142),

and in recent time has been connected with the names of McLeod Campbell in Scotland and Horace Bushnell in America. With all that may be said of the inadequacies of this theory, one thing is certain, that whatever else the death of Christ may mean—and the present writer believes it means more—it does accomplish one thing which must be true of any adequate theory of the atonement; it lifts into clear and unmistakable emphasis the unconquerable love of God for men.

This historical survey is all too short and yet I am led to feel that it demonstrates how inevitable it is that in every age men must seek to enter in and understand what this event, the death of Jesus Christ, is to mean to them. They have come to feel that it is the climactic event in human history, and that they must understand it just so far as it is possible. So I am led to ask the same old question again, What may the death of Christ mean to us? What interest, in other words, have we to-day in the death of Christ?

In approaching this question much depends on the starting-point, and of all possible starting-points the one which helps me most is the declaration of Paul that "God was in Christ reconciling the world to himself" (2 Cor. 5. 19). This makes forever impossible any theory of the atonement such as that expressed by Isaac Watts in his stanza:

> "Rich were the drops of Jesus' blood
> Which calmed God's frowning face,
> That sprinkled o'er the burning throne
> And turned the wrath to grace."

The difficulty with all such theories is the inference that *God had to be made willing* to forgive men and receive them back to himself by the voluntary sacrifice of Christ. Is there any wonder that a little girl should have exclaimed when such a thought was presented to her, "I love Jesus, but I hate God"? Every thought we have about the death of Christ must assert that God was in what Jesus endured and suffered as completely as Jesus himself. Jesus Christ was expressing in our world and in human terms what God had always felt. It was God who so loved the world that he initiated the process by which the reconciliation between man and himself might take place. In "the fullness of time" God sent his Son that what he had always meant might be completely revealed.

There is another misconception which must be removed before it is possible to proceed further. It may be put in the form of a quotation from one of our American journals of religion. A reader asks this question, "If God forgave sins to men who repented and turned to him all through the Old Testament dispensation, why was it necessary for Christ to come and give himself as a sacrifice for our sins?" This was a very sensible question, but here is the answer: "In a very real sense God did not forgive sins to repentant Old Testament sinners. He only 'winked' at them (Acts 17. 30, A. V.), or 'overlooked' them, as the Revised Version puts it. He merely 'passed over' them in forbearance (Rom. 3. 25) until Christ died on the cross and then retroactively he could forgive them. . . . If Christ had not died, men of olden times could never have been saved." How unreal! That word "retroactively"—where have we any statement in the Bible that gives any ground for such a conception? How cheap this idea of forgiveness is! If salvation through forgiveness means a new life of fellowship

with God and not merely being saved from the consequences of sin, these men of old were living without
the most precious of all the experiences a human soul
can know. If they were not saved from their sins and
were not in fellowship with God, what did they have
of which they give every evidence of being so thankful? All this is in contradiction to many statements
in the Old Testament. We need only turn to Psalm
103. 3, where we find the statement, "Who forgiveth
all thine iniquities; who healeth all thy diseases." And
again in Psalm 86. 5:

"For thou, Lord, art good, and ready to forgive;
 And abundant in loving-kindness unto all them that
     call upon thee."

There are, of course, many other similar passages. It
was a present experience for these men or it was nothing, and we can scarcely imagine a perversion of
Scripture more misleading than when the forgiving
love of God is made to wait upon the death of Christ,
when in reality God's heart was always ready to forgive and did actually forgive those who were repentant throughout the Old Testament period.

I fear the last paragraph has been rather disconcerting to some who would not be willing to travel
the whole distance with the one who answered the
question asked by the reader just quoted. If God
could and did forgive before Christ died for sinners,
what is there to say about that death? What function has it to perform when we are told that Jesus
Christ came to die for the sins of the world and then
learn that forgiveness was experienced by men long
before the sacrifice of Calvary? There is no answer
to this question from the standpoint of those who

hold that God was not able for some reason to forgive until after the death of Christ, that there was a bar to his forgiveness which could only be removed by the sacrifice of his Son. The only satisfying answer must be based on considerations of a very different character, considerations which have been suggested in our attempt to interpret Jesus' words and deeds as he approached his crowning sacrifice, but which must now be developed further.

There can be little doubt that the death of Christ made possible what was impossible until that supreme event. The kingdom of God, such a kingdom as Jesus planned, of which he was the inaugurator, could not be founded without sacrifice. It must reach down to the depths of human experience so that Jesus might be able to save to the uttermost them that came to him. All other religious movements the world has ever seen, even the greatest and most profound, were relatively superficial compared with the movement inaugurated by Jesus. His kingdom was founded on love, love at its uttermost limit of devotion and sacrifice. Nothing has ever been known like it, so no other movement can compare with it. It was only when Jesus Christ came and was able to make such a complete revelation of the heart of God that the "fullness of time" had come and this new religion could be launched successfully.

But before we can realize the meaning of the founding of a kingdom on vicarious sacrifice, we must see a little more clearly what was revealed in that sacrifice. It was to be a kingdom of human beings, men and women who were alienated from God. They must be brought back and there must be a restoration of the relation between God and man which had been broken by sin. To accomplish this was the aim of the coming of Jesus Christ. What did it involve? It certainly must include two things. Man must be made to realize the breadth and the depth of the love of God for men, and, this must be done in such a manner that the awfulness of sin should stand out in all its stark horror. And these things the death of Christ does. We can see this as we interpret his death in the light of his teaching and his life. This will make us careful not to make too great a difference between the life which Jesus lived and the death he died. His whole experience is of a piece and cannot be torn in two without peril. Jesus lived vicariously as he died vicariously. The meaning of his death only stands out the more wonderfully when it is interpreted by his words and his unselfish devotion to men and women from the beginning of his career to the end.

When Jesus gave up his life on the cross the way was open as it had never been before to know what love really means. Here for a moment the skies were torn apart and we caught a glimpse of the eternal verities. Here was Jesus suffering and dying, exhibiting the loving heart of God, suffering because of sin and longing with an intensity even to death that men might be reconciled and return to their Father. But more than that, here was what sin could do; it had broken the heart of God himself, and in Jesus we have a terrible glimpse of the suffering of God and realize that sin is a far worse thing than we had ever imagined. If it could cause God so great an agony, what must it be? But if in all his revulsion against sin God could send his Son to suffer and die, what love must be at the heart of the universe! Here is where men's hearts have been broken and healed at the same time. They have seen themselves as sinners, black and despicable, but even more clearly they have seen God, not only as the matchlessly pure, but as the ever-loving Father, eager for them to come back to him.

So I conclude that the sacrifice of Jesus Christ was necessary because of what God purposed to accomplish by it. As a Father his uttermost desire was that men might be brought back into fellowship with him. To accomplish this they must never forget that he loved them and that he loved them to the extent of the most terrible sacrifice he could make. But there was still another factor, essential if the quality of his relations with men were to be kept on the highest level of moral concern, and that was that men in the very process of realizing the depth of the love of God in Christ and in the very experience of forgiveness should recognize just as clearly how deeply they had wounded the heart of God, what suffering it had cost and was still costing him. Forgiveness must be free if it is real forgiveness at all, but it is always costly to the one who forgives. God's forgiveness must not be held cheap even if it is free. These values the sacrifice of Jesus Christ conserved completely and most effectively. The cross is the most adequate symbol of our religion, and the death of Christ on Calvary the central fact in the history of the world. Before that supreme event took place the moral content of forgiveness and the abounding gratitude of the one forgiven could not be what they were when their meaning is measured by the fullness of love and sacrifice shown on the cross.

Finally, the question may arise, Have we not had other wonderful exhibitions of self-sacrifice, where men have given themselves even to death that friends and loved ones might be saved from suffering and death, or might receive some prized boon? Without doubt this is true, and he would be a poor Christian who in the light of Calvary cannot with clear vision and enthusiastic admiration appreciate and almost reverence every illustration of heroism of which he reads or hears. But there is a difference, a difference so marked that the world has registered a thousand times its verdict that here is love supreme, giving itself in such absolute devotion and self-forgetting service that no other act has ever been able to compare with it. It seems to gather up in one sublime deed all that every act of self-sacrifice points to and illustrates in wonderful but lesser fashion. The reason for this is not far to seek for the Christian. It is a unique sacrifice because Jesus Christ is unique. He is related to God in such an intimate manner that what he does is as if God were performing the deed himself through the instrumentality of flesh and blood. This can be said of no other of the sons of men. This Son of man who is at the same time Son of God, being God clothed in human flesh and sharing our experiences, could do what none of his lesser brethren could accomplish. We stand off and wonder and then sink down in gratitude that thus completely he showed us God as our Father whose will is that all should come through Christ to him and be saved.

CHAPTER XVIII

WHAT BECOMES OF A MAN WHEN HE DIES?

WHAT becomes of a man when he dies? We take it for granted that he must die, and rarely, if ever, ask ourselves how life would seem if it should happen that death no longer stared us in the face. This thought was first suggested to me by an able and saintly minister, whose conclusion was that life would be intolerable if there should be no ending of our earthly career. Look at it closely, with all our clinging to life would we want it indefinitely prolonged? Suppose we could go on living here without old age, sickness, suffering, sorrow, financial loss, disappointment, hardship, poverty, all of which are looked upon as enemies of happiness and from which we turn away. What would happen if we could go on living and living through the eternities without these features which mar the lot of our life on earth? Would we want it thus prolonged under such conditions? I am afraid many would, but the result would be most deplorable. Undoubtedly their condition would be one which no strong man would desire. They would undoubtedly sink into a stupor of satisfaction which would cause life to lose its meaning. This could scarcely be prevented; it would be the inevitable result of a prolongation of life forever on the earth without any of the difficulties and ills which now surround us.

While it is not noticed when young, the experience which comes to all those who are in mature life and beyond is that age lays its hand upon us and draws us rapidly toward the end when our earthly life will be terminated. Is old age beautiful and delightful to contemplate? Can we all say with Robert Browning, "Grow old along with me, the best is yet to be, the last of life for which the first was made"? I know one woman of saintly life and character who has been repeating these lines for years, whose hope of immortality is bright and clear, and yet who testifies that in spite of it all she does not like old age. There are many beautiful things about it and yet, when we consider how many suffer and that old age for many others means a weakening not only of the physical powers but also of the mind, the prospect is not inviting to say the least. But suppose we could live on without growing old and just in our prime, what would be our attitude? The answer comes that the incentive which makes life interesting, which gives it its meaning, would be lost, and we would be less than the men and women we are to-day.

But while men face death as inevitable, they cling to life and want a continuance of it. It may not completely satisfy, it may be surrounded by many things which render it scarcely worth living, and yet there is this eagerness which cannot be quenched. Men want life and more life, and will not be satisfied with anything they have here below. So imperious is this unsatisfied longing that most of the people in the world in all ages have looked forward to another life on the other side of death. The kind of life has differed greatly in the imagination of those who have cherished these dreams, but the fact itself is sufficient testimony to the peristence of the hope of immortality in the breasts of men.

It is this very dissatisfaction with what is and the anticipation of what may be that drive men out of their lethargy and give them a hope of more of the best things which they have seen and experienced and tasted here. Without these things it would scarcely be possible to imagine that humanity could hold up under the strain and be able to take the shocks of life as bravely as they do. The very values which life possesses imply in many cases the continuance of life. Its cessation would do away with these values entirely, and when the full significance of what is being done has been appreciated, it would dull the edge of existence and life would be lived on a lower plane. Men would not have the grit and the determination to fight it out or to bear the strain of illness or misfortune.

But what of those who to-day do not have the hope of immortality? In this realm, as in others, there are abnormal men and women as well as those who are normal. The normal man or woman, if we may learn any lesson at all from the whole history of the human race, holds fast to certain values, values which involve a continuance of life out in the regions beyond. While it is true that an individual here and there may be able to live his life bravely with no hope of immortality, it is exceedingly doubtful whether a great group of men in the complexity of life to-day could sustain themselves were they deprived of this hope and the full significance of their want should gradually become apparent to them. The important fact is that while there have been scoffers and unbelievers in immortality in many countries and in various religions, the great mass of men, educated and uneducated, cultured and uncultured, of all races cling with a tenacity which cannot be gainsaid to a belief that when a man dies, somewhere, somehow, in some form, he will live again.

Are these undying hopes which men cherish anything more than dreams? Is there any assurance of immortality which may comfort the soul and give it the kind of conviction from which nothing can tear men away? Is there such a thing as a demonstration of the life beyond on which we may rest with utter security? Coming directly to a positive answer, there is probably no doubt in the minds of thinking men and women to-day that there is no proof or demonstration of immortality. Strange, is it not, that while this is true, men cling to immortality as tenaciously to-day as in any time in the whole history of mankind? There is something, then, beyond proof of a formal kind and beyond the demonstration which mathematics furnishes which is able to hold the mind of man so securely that what might seem to be facts on the other side cannot make them waver in their assurance.

This has been said with full knowledge of the widespread revival of spiritualism which has followed in the wake of the war. Thousands upon thousands of young men in the flower of their career were cut off and parents and friends were caused to think about the life beyond and the possibility of immortality with an eagerness which only such an experience could arouse. It is not surprising, then, that there should have been a revival of spiritualism. The attempt is made to come into touch with the other world so that we may have a kind of physical contact with those who have gone on before. The hope is expressed that the spiritual world may become sensibly apparent to men and women living on this side of death. It is not possible in a study such as this to go into the details of the problem of spiritualism. All we can do is to state what has been concluded by many students, a conclusion which fits in better with the Christian viewpoint than that which the spiritualists take. In brief it is this: that nothing has been proved positively or negatively. We must recognize that insofar as our senses are involved, we are not dealing with the spiritual world at all. About as far as these so-called spiritualists get is a thin, vaporous, attenuated, material substance, which they speak of as the materialization of the spiritual. But insofar as what we are looking at in a spiritualistic seance is material it is not spiritual. No matter how thin or vaporous it may be it is still matter and not spirit, for the two belong to different realms, and one cannot be transfused or transformed into the other without the loss of its essential properties. Very interesting things have been done by these spiritualists. They have doubtless gone as far as it is possible for the human mind to penetrate, but, after all, science or pseudo-science cannot prove anything concerning the spiritual one way or the other. In other words, everything that these mediums have done has neither proved nor disproved immortality.

If this be true, what, then, is the value of the so-called proofs of immortality? I do not know how it could be put more concisely or clearly than by Professor George Galloway: "The various proofs Plato offers for immortality are ways of justifying the verdict of the moral consciousness." That is, men and women at their best testify to an unquenchable belief that this life is not all. They believe that there must be some kind of fruition in another life which is not possible in this. We try to justify this hope by every means in our power, but when we have gone the full distance we cannot conclude that it is irrational for doubt to arise in the mind of one who does not have the conviction as strongly as ourselves.

It may be well to look at some of these arguments. We may go to Plato, who, in the words of Professor George Foot Moore, was so immersed in the thought of immortality that he said "explicitly or implicitly pretty much all that has ever been said on the subject." There are four arguments which he used with great effectiveness. The first was the argument from the universality of the belief in some kind of existence after this life. The second was the argument from the moral necessity of retribution. Men everywhere have felt that the good things of life were not evenly distributed, that is, in accord with justice or the needs of men. It is a topsy-turvy universe in which we live, but it would be positively crazy unless we could be sure that somehow, somewhere right would be done and justice would be meted out in exact accord with worth and merit. One needs only to suggest the nature of this argument to discover how strong it is. Men will not believe that the ultimate meaning of the universe is expressed in the conditions which we find around us now. So long as they believe in God, a God of love and a God of justice, they will look forward to the day when there shall be a display of that love which distributes its recompense in accord with justice and consideration for the best interests of all. The third argument is that from the aspirations of the human soul. How can we account for the fact that men and women, the best men and women who have ever lived, believed that their life received added value and meaning by this desire for something better and purer and holier than anything which this earth can provide? Surely, there must be a beyond where righteousness shall flourish, if there be a God at all, who is bound to see to it that right prevails. The last of these Platonic arguments is the essential nature of the human soul itself. Plato believed that there was something immortal about the human soul, something which inherently prevented it from being destroyed. It was fitted for a life beyond this, and nothing that could happen would destroy its inner texture and make it impossible to inherit the life which its nature showed it was capable of enjoying. When one reads these arguments and ponders on them, their force instead of diminishing becomes stronger as the years pass by. There can be no doubt that they have helped to buttress the hope of immortality which men find deeply lodged in their breasts. But yet they are not proofs, only reasons which the human mind and heart are able to assemble in the intense desire to justify the expectation and aspiration which lie firmly rooted in their depths.

The Christian hope of immortality had comparatively little to build upon in the Old Testament. In the early days it was Egypt that developed the hope of immortality and clothed it in manifold forms. So deeply dyed in immortality was the thought of the Egyptians that it stands out as the most important of all the religious conceptions of this remarkable people. Strange to say, those who were neighbors of the Egyptians on the east, the Babylonians and the Assyrians and other representatives of the Semitic race, did not share their belief in immortality. These

Semites progressed a very short distance beyond an exceedingly hazy belief that men lived in the next life a most undesirable existence. They went to a place called Sheol, where there was no distinction between good men and bad men and very little between those who were prosperous on this earth and those who were poor. Sheol was a common receptacle for all mankind, but the life lived was most unbearable. Inhabitants of this region, which was down under the surface of the earth, were virtually shades, with a kind of dreamy existence in which nothing was worth while. This subterranean region was dark and clammy and dusty. The most surprising part of it all was that it was not under the control of the gods to whom men prayed while they lived on earth. This was the background inherited by the Hebrew people, and not much more was added until toward the close of the Old Testament period. Almost all a Hebrew could hope for was that he might live many years and leave behind him a large family in whom he would have his immortality. He desired to stay here as long as possible, for there was nothing desirable in the future. When he passed away, full of years and blessed by children and grandchildren who looked upon him as their great father and benefactor, he could approach the future with as much equanimity as was possible with the meager conception of immortality which was his. It is clearly impossible here to trace the steps away from the crudeness of this early view. Suffice it to say that in the late Old Testament period the individual began to come to his own. Men became conscious of their own individuality as separate and distinct from the family and the clan. They learned to have communion with God, and this brought a change.   Communion with the Creator of the universe was looked upon by these saints as the most precious thing in their experience, and the most significant thing about it was that they could not believe it would ever end.   Here was the germ of immortality which later bore such plenteous fruit.

Fellowship with God was a relationship which they felt would be as unending as the eternal God himself. Thus did the hope of immortality arise and grow in the Old Testament period.   But even at its very best little progress was made, so that it would be correctly stated by Paul that Jesus Christ brought life and immortality to light through the gospel.   What was the contribution Jesus made to this conception?   He lived in contact with the spiritual world, he literally lived the eternal life, whose quality was such that no one could imagine that it could end.   On the basis of his own experience Jesus pointed toward the same kind of life as a natural expectation for others.   He was more concerned with life than with anything else. We find him always in opposition to death.   This was his accepted task.   He saw mental and spiritual death around him everywhere and gave life in its place.   He himself died, but the strongest conviction the disciples had about Jesus when they went out to preach his Name was that he had overcome death in his own person.   He appeared to them as the Lord of Life. He convinced his disciples that it was the same Jesus with whom they had walked in Galilee who appeared to them and made them sure that he was alive.   Our Christian view of immortality is the gift of Jesus Christ, a gift which came out of the quality of life which he lived.   His life had the touch of the eternal on it and, in addition, he was able to convince his disciples that physical death could not hold him as it had held other members of the human family. They became preachers of the resurrection, not only of Christ, but of all those who shared his life.

What do we know about the life beyond? No religion has succeeded in making eternal life so real as has Christianity. With this in mind it may be a surprise to discover that Christianity says less than many other religions about the nature of that life which we are to live in the future. We may say certain things and be quite sure we are right. It is everlasting life, but that alone would help us very little. The chief contribution that word makes is that, whatever good there may be in the world to come, we shall never be in dread that the experience will terminate in something less desirable. But far more important is the emphasis which Christianity lays upon the quality of the life. In the New Testament it is called eternal life, and the word "eternal" must be interpreted not as mere lasting forever but as that which partakes of a peculiar quality, like that which we think of whenever our minds turn to Jesus Christ. It is the kind of life he lived that must fill our consciousness if we are to get any justifiable idea of heaven.

We must also recognize that this life is to be in fellowship with Christ and that that fellowship will bring about a likeness to him which, after all, is one of the greatest boons which can ever come to a Christian. We hear John say, "It is not yet made manifest what we shall be. We know that, if he shall be manifested, we shall be like him; for we shall see him even as he is." A great many foolish things have been said about heaven. How thankful we ought to be that the New Testament is silent on many points where other religions and even Christians have tried to be very particular in their descriptions. A great deal is said concerning the recognition of relatives and friends. I have no doubt that being like Jesus means that we shall remain persons, and one of the essential things in personality is fellowship, and fellowship is impossible without recognition. I cannot see how we can go very far astray by believing that we may have fellowship with our friends in the world of the future, but there are many who have allowed this thought to be so important that it has almost drowned out the supreme fact in the Christian attitude toward the future. They have so lost perspective that they do not see that everything in the hereafter must be interpreted in the light of the supreme relationship which we are to have with Jesus Christ.

There can be no doubt that in the world to come the sorrows and the sins which have marred human life here shall be conspicuous by their absence. There must be peace and joy as men in righteousness have fellowship one with another. We shall then know what a truly unselfish life is as we experience it in our own conduct through fellowship with Christ himself. We might go on adding a few features such as have been mentioned, and there are sufficient of these to thrill the human heart as it looks forward to that companionship and to that service. But beyond this we know very little. Paul tells us, in a quotation, to be sure, but a quotation which he makes his own, "Eye hath not seen, nor ear heard, neither have entered into the heart of man, the things which God has prepared for them that love him." Very mercifully the details have not been filled in. We could not understand them even though they were written down as

looked upon as dangerous is that a man may say to himself that there is little reason to be especially concerned about his sins if God is willing to receive him back on repentance at any time. Why, then, should we urge the necessity of repentance here and now? Surely, a man will repent when he sees things as they are in the next world. Yes, I suppose if a man should stand on the brink of an awful fate, his immediate impulse would be to do anything he could to escape it. Why would he not repent when he faces the facts as they are? But the question which arises is, Would this be real repentance at all? Would it not, rather, be the desire to escape a dreadful fate? The consequences of sin yawn before him and he seeks to escape, but would there be any ethical content in it at all? Would it not be merely the natural desire to save oneself from an awful doom? The value of a moral decision lies in the fact that an argument can be put up on the other side, that reasons can be given for doing the thing which one is tempted to do, even though there may be other good reasons for not doing it. It may be of great immediate advantage for one to do what the temptation suggests. There may be pleasure in it, or gain, or influence, or personal satisfaction, things which gratify and please. And yet all the way through the man himself would know that it was wrong to do that thing. No moral decision which is worth anything can be made without this necessity of choosing between two courses, not on the basis that either one of them brings an immediate gain or an immediate loss, but because one of these things is right and the other is wrong. A moral decision is one where the arguments may be even more numerous on the one side than on the other, and yet in spite of much that would lead in the opposite direction the decision is made to do the right because it is right, irrespective of advantages which might come in doing the other thing. It means following the best one knows under all circumstances, to be with Jesus Christ no matter where it leads. Now we come to the important point that it is in just the kind of world in which we live that such a decision can be made at its best. There is the element of risk. We make a venture on the side of the morally good in spite of many things which might be brought up to our advantage on the other side. If we saw clearly the consequences of what we are doing we might be led to decide on the basis of these consequences. Even as it is in this life of ours, we may see consequences, but in many cases, and these are the significant ones, the decisions we are called upon to make are those in which we can see only a short distance ahead and are led to make our decision on the basis of our sense of what is right as contrasted with what is wrong, on the side of God instead of on the side of evil. No other world that could be imagined would offer the opportunity to reach the kind of decision which makes for character, and do it so advantageously, as the world in which we live.

But there is more to it than this. One of the surest facts of the moral life is that character tends increasingly to become fixed. This is a matter of common observation. Youth is the plastic period. Most men and women make their decisions for character early in life, and when these decisions are made, the character tends to become more fixed as the years and decades pass. So that when we find a man of forty or fifty years of age we might say that in ninety-nine cases out of a hundred his character is fixed for good, whether it be good or whether it be evil. We hesitate very greatly to say this when we think of the many who have chosen badly and are on the downward path. This, however, is only the other side of that more wonderful truth that, when a man starts to do well and makes the decision of his life in favor of the best he knows, his character tends to become fixed as the years go by, until when he has become mature and approaches the period of old age we might say that that man could be surely counted upon to be pure and noble and upright. His character has become fixed in goodness.

I cannot see anything in the other world which would alter this psychological law, and this applies both to good and evil. The longer we study the problem the more true it seems that this world is a place of moral probation. As Robert Browning puts it, this world is

"Machinery just meant to give thy soul its bent,
Try thee and send thee forth sufficiently impressed."

This world is not so much a place where character becomes a finished product as it is where we give character its direction, by making the choices which ultimately result in fixed habits of good or bad. We do actually decide its bent and give life its meaning, and, so far as my view is concerned, I cannot see that the conditions of human life would be so changed that this law would be altered no matter how many worlds a man passed through. All this leads naturally to the conclusion that this life is of tremendous importance, and that we are placed in this world in order to find the right way and walk in it and thus give direction to the development of our character through the eternities. Thus the difficulty is not with God and his mercy; it is with man. He becomes fixed in character as the years pass and thus places himself beyond the region where God can do for him what he would; that is, provided the man has taken the wrong path.

Now, what shall be said about punishment? We rebel at the word punishment, probably very largely because it seems so arbitrary. It might even be put in words like this: "If we are not careful, God will get us." And whenever anyone holds a theory which can be expressed in these or similar words the whole idea of punishment becomes hateful. God never "gets" us in that sense. He is not out trying to find men who stumble and do wrong and then gloat over the fact that he has found them in an unfortunate condition and therefore can wreak his vengeance on them. No, but when a man deliberately turns against God and his plan for life and identifies himself with his own self-will and its utter selfishness, he brings upon himself the revulsion of God against evil, the evil with which the man has identified himself. God can only turn against such a man. This is divine retribution, this is punishment, a very different thing from the vindictive attitude which sometimes is made to be that of God toward those who sin. God is a grieving and not a vindictive God, and when we fall into his hands it is into the hands of one whose attitude toward us would have been and is even now an attitude of love, but whose actual reaction toward sin makes it necessary for him to withdraw his presence and to treat the sinner in the way in which his deliberate choice has made necessary. When love is sinned against it does not cease to be love, but it is rendered helpless to do its typical work in the life of any man.

But will such an attitude on the part of God continue through the eternities? Sometimes it has seemed to the writer that there is among Christian teachers a very strenuous insistence on morality here in this life, and at the same time a failure to realize that the only worthy conception of the future life is one where the ethical shall be given as important a place as in the life we live now. Sometimes it would seem as though God would be more lenient toward sin there than he is here, that somehow he can do in another life what he cannot do in this. But if we are to be thoroughly ethical, we must preserve the ethical attitude throughout the universe. If we do not do so, we run the danger of concluding that our moral concern is not so important as it might be, for God himself may become more lax in another world than he is in his relationship with us here. Whatever other things Christianity is, there is always one thing to be said, that it cannot be understood at all except as built upon a moral foundation. This foundation must sustain everything in God's universe with no exception whatsoever.

But some will say that punishment must always be remedial. I am quite sure that if God could make it so, it would be so. We cannot possibly think of him from a Christian standpoint as in any sense vindictive. To be the God of love every contact with man must be one through which he hopes to bring out the best in the life of man, and thus even his punishments might prove remedial. He is far more anxious about the salvation of the last sinner than we are. But we must remember the awful fact that, whatever the one who administers the punishment may do, or whatever his attitude may be, and with whatever kindly intent the punishment is inflicted, it may not prove to be remedial in all cases. The attitude of the one who is punished determines the nature of that punishment, providing the one administering it is not vindictive and is constantly hoping that whatever is done may result in a new life in the one upon whom it is necessary to visit the punishment. God is not to be looked upon as trying to get even with anyone, but the side we often forget is that, with the fixity of character we see on every hand, atrophy takes place in the moral realm as well as in the physical and intellectual. We have done away with a hell of fire and brimstone. But, none the less, there is still the fact that men do turn away from God and bring down punishment upon their heads, with a result which ultimately is just as terrible as was ever pictured in the day of realistic tortures for the damned. Men are separated from God. The good that is in man dwindles and dwindles until even the desire for what is better disappears. A creature of whom these statements can be made is in a hell deeper and more abysmal than any lurid hell which was pictured in the age when fire and brimstone were taken literally. Will such punishment or such a condition of separation from God be everlasting? I do not know very well what the word "everlasting" means. Whenever I try to think about it, it escapes me. What I am concerned about is the quality of life or existence, and here we have an existence with everything good eliminated, and this is enough for me to know. Hope seems almost excluded from such a life by the very conditions of its existence.

Let us realize that the most serious and terrible things that have ever been said in human history about the fate of the wicked came from Jesus Christ himself, the sinless and pure Son of God. He saw evil as it was more clearly than any who have trod our planet, and it was he who declared that the judgment of God must fall on those who finally turn away from him and reject his love and his mercy.

Who are these I have been speaking of? It is not for me or for any human being to say. We are not the judges, but I am sure that there will be nothing arbitrary about it, nor will there be any surprises. We are told that Judas "went to his own place"; so will every one of us, and there are at bottom only two directions in which men are traveling, the direction of self-will and the direction of service, adhesion to one's lower nature or to the higher. God is using every inducement short of compulsion to lead men into the path of honor and truth and purity and unselfishness and service, and the tragedy of tragedies in the universe is that some turn away. We cannot escape the fact if we look at life unflinchingly. All we can do is to warn men that sin is dreadful and does nothing but destroy. It is an awful fact to contemplate what ultimately will happen to those who, in face of opportunities to the contrary, give themselves to that which will draw them away from right and God. Is there not another side? Is there no hope for those who die unrepentant? I wonder whether many of us have realized that this is more of a problem for God than for us. He is a Father, whose heart is full of compassion and love, who is far more desirous of the salvation of the sinner than we can be. The best thing for us is to leave things in his hands, knowing that his children are safer there than anywhere we can imagine. His mercy is unbounded and the slightest turn of the heart toward real repentance will be eagerly noted. God would cease to be Father were this not his attitude. But with all this, our duty lies clear. Sin is dreadful and its consequences sure. We cannot proclaim the gospel of Jesus Christ without making clear the New Testament emphasis on the character of sin and what it does, and this has been the attempt in this discussion.

CHAPTER XX

WHY DO MEN PRAY?

THE question assumes that men do pray, and such is the fact. In all lands and in all ages from the very earliest times men have believed that there is some power higher than themselves to whom they are related and with whom they can communicate. This is a perfectly normal experience; the man who does not pray is abnormal. It is he who is running contrary to the prevalent tendency in human nature. It is he upon whom rests the burden of proof to show that there is reason why men should not give themselves to the practice which we call prayer.

The prayer of the more primitive peoples is very instructive. It must be called prayer even though the circle of interests and the objects desired are purely physical and material. Prayer under these conditions has only begun to fathom the depths of what prayer may be, but it is very clear that the essential element is recognized, that man may enter into communication with the unseen powers which control his destiny. The prayer of these simple-minded people also shows several of the dangers to which we ourselves are liable in prayer. There is a tendency to look upon the utterance of the name of the Spirit or Deity as giving the worshiper a kind of lien or purchase on his good will. They believe that the mere repetition of a request is potent to bring about the effect desired. They have learned a hidden and powerful secret. They have discovered the charm or spell by which ends could be gained because of the magic power which the very repetition of the words contained. Prayer in that case becomes an instrument in the hands of men of controlling destiny, not so much because the divine power listened and was willing to grant the request desired, but because the repetition of the prayer itself is potent in coercing the Deity and bringing the end about almost mechanically. The fact is that in this case prayer is no longer in the realm of religion. It has become an agency of magic, wherein the essential element is the power of the repetition of the words to bring about the end desired irrespective of the will of the higher power concerned. It has become a spell instead of a prayer.

The same danger is suggested by an illuminated sign which greeted the visitor to one of the great religious celebrations of recent years. This sign contained the words, "Prayer Releases Power." I suppose very few thought anything about the sign except that it declared what they had heard many times from Christian pulpits, and yet just as it stands it does not ring true. The contrast may be realized by asking the question, Does prayer release power, or is it God who releases power? Everyone would quickly answer that it is God, and that God releases power in answer to prayer. This, of course, is just what we all believe, but sometimes we are in danger of seeming at least to mean that the very act of repeating the words of prayer is effective to bring about the object desired. We frequently hear children, and even grown-ups, declare that they have "said their prayers," as if there were some value in the saying of these words. What we need to be reminded of is that prayer is always communication with God and that the repetition of words is only a means to that end, as are words in conversation between ourselves. What is accomplished through prayer does not come by the repetition of words but by God, who is able to do certain things because in prayer the minds and hearts of men are open to what otherwise would be an impossibility, even to God himself. If prayer were only the repetition of words, it would become little more than soliloquy, talking to oneself, using magic words which have come down out of the past and are supposed to be sacred and efficacious merely because of the tradition that they have been used by holy men in the past to bring about desired results.

Accordingly, does prayer always imply a belief in God or some higher power? The answer must be in the affirmative. Is there, then, no such thing as meditation? Without doubt meditation is one of the most useful of practices, but it is not prayer unless it becomes a method of communing with the great God above, and then it becomes prayer in reality. The question may also be raised, Is there not such a thing as communion with nature? Undoubtedly there is, and it lies very close to prayer, and may pass over into prayer when one through nature realizes the presence of nature's God. But let us remember and insist upon it that prayer always has as its essential ingredient communion with an objective power whom we as Christians know as God.

But what about the investigations which have been made in the psychology of prayer? It is admitted that they are of very high importance and exceedingly helpful. We need to know the conditions under which prayer can most helpfully be practiced. We need to know the mental and spiritual laws which govern the inner life and control the movement of the mind and heart toward the object of faith. These laws cannot be neglected, and to disregard them is to court spiritual impotence and emptiness. We must remember, however, that the psychology of prayer as psychology cannot deal with that which is most essential to prayer, the fact of the presence of God. This goes beyond the possibility of what the science of psychology may accomplish. The temptation on the part of certain psychologists is to lay such emphasis on the subjective elements in prayer that they are led to ask the question whether there is anything more to prayer than simply this psychological aspect. The danger lies in attempting by this process of abstraction to come to conclusions about prayer without taking into account the essential fact of God. Without this factor there would be no mental facts with which the psychologist could deal. Prayer would cease to be an influence in men's lives if they did not continue to feel that in its exercise they were in the presence of a God who heard what they said. Men might turn to meditation, as so many have done, but they would surely cease to pray and in sincerity of heart would declare that it is a very different practice from that to which they gave themselves when they believed in God and could realize his presence in those moments when the exercise of prayer was as vital as anything in their experience.

But when all this has been said the difficulties concerning prayer still remain. This is not a damaging admission. I feel perfectly convinced that no endeavor on the part of students to clear away all the difficulties will succeed if one were compelled to put off the habit of prayer until his questions were answered. He would no more pray than he would eat or trust his neighbor or fall in love, if it were necessary for him to settle all the perplexities which adhere to each one of these acts and attitudes. So far as he can find satisfying answers to his questions, they will come more through the life of prayer itself than in any other way. There is a logic of the devotional life as well as the logic of the syllogism and of our purely intellectual processes, and this can be appreciated only by living the life of prayer itself.

One of the questions which always emerge when prayer is mentioned is, Why pray when we believe God knows all?—how unnecessary it is! Why should we seek to bring things to God's attention when he who is the All-Wise One knows all these things already? The only sufficient answer is that this is the only kind of God worth praying to. Our God is not an ignorant God. He does not have to be informed as to what is going on in his universe. It is true that he knows all that is taking place when we go to him in prayer— that is the very reason we go to him. We bring ourselves, with all our hopes and aspirations, our weaknesses and sins, our desires and needs, to One who is able to deal with them because he knows the entire situation far better than we do. This consideration is likely to change the definition of prayer for many. It becomes a very different thing from what is so often conceived of as prayer. We come to One who knows everything about ourselves and pour our hearts out before him, not for the sake of informing him of things which he does not know but to enable him to do what otherwise would be impossible, even for the omnipotent God. Thus prayer is in a very real sense the

channel of communication between God and ourselves, and our duty is to keep this channel open and
unclogged so that we may come into his presence and
receive from him what we need as often as that need
arises.

Does prayer make any difference with God? If it
did not, he would be less than a personal God, for to
be personal means among other things to be affected
by personal relationships. God responds to the personal touch. No more than a mother does God need
to be persuaded to be merciful or kind. He is the
God of love and tenderness, and praying can never
make him more so. Prayer in a very true and deep
sense is a confession on our part that we can trust
him to be what he is. In response to that trust God
can do for us what otherwise would be impossible.
The realm of personal relationships and the response
of heart to heart is the only realm in which character
can grow, whether they be the relationships which we
have with one another or with God.

But if prayer makes a difference with God, what
becomes of natural law? Well, what becomes of natural law when I do something for you, something
which I would never have thought of doing if you had
not asked me to do you a favor? Is God more helpless in his universe than his creatures are? What we
must always remember is that God is a God of law
and order, and does not break his law or disrupt the
order which he has ordained. God works among
possibilities and never beyond them. This means that
it is quite possible to ask foolish things of God and
things which are either impossible or which have no
value in the wide outreach of the Kingdom. God has
so constituted the universe that he cannot cause an

event to be as if it had not taken place. A fact is inescapable even for God. Such things are not among the objects which can reasonably be brought into the list of requests to be made of God, and so on through a great many other impossibilities. We cannot ask of God to make a bad man good against the bad man's will. This is a moral impossibility. It would be a disruption of the moral universe if such a thing could happen. What we need to learn is that, after we have made all our requests, the last statement to be made in any Christian prayer is that which was expressed by Jesus when he said, "Not my will, but thine be done." If it was necessary for him to make such a statement, how much more so for us, in our ignorance and sin, in our inability to realize the significance of many situations in which we find ourselves!

What about answers to prayers? Undoubtedly very many good Christian people have been greatly troubled at this point. And those who are more skeptically inclined have been tempted to become cynical when they discover so many things which are declared to be answers to prayer which they themselves could account for in a perfectly natural manner. It has often seemed to such on-lookers that it is almost presumptuous to declare that such and such an event took place in answer to prayer, when it is quite evident that there are a dozen contingencies and possibilities which have not been taken into consideration when such a conclusion was reached. Are we not justified in agreeing with the scientific and also Christian conclusion that in the nature of the case there can be no scientific verification of answers to prayer? This does not mean that prayers are not answered, nor does it mean that there may not be a hundred times in a man's life when he feels certain that what has taken place has come because God had heard the prayer of a righteous man and has accomplished what would have been otherwise impossible. It only means that we should be careful about declaring that we know without peradventure of a doubt that this or that took place because this or that prayer was answered directly in this manner. We do not know much about many things which are taking place around us, so we should hesitate to be oversure about specific answers to specific prayers. This need not in any way dull the edge of our conviction that were it not for prayer we would not be Christians, were it not for prayer God's kingdom could not come, were it not for prayer many heartaches could not be healed, and were it not for prayer many events in our world would take a very different turn from that which they have actually taken. God does hear and answer prayer, so that we should bring all our needs to him as a Father who desires the best for his children.

But after we have said all that is necessary concerning answers to prayer and our belief in them, one wonders whether we are not, after all, making what is secondary of primary importance. Let us use a human analogy. What is the valued element in our friendships? Is it what we get out of them or the actual union of soul with soul which they imply? Is not the fellowship itself that element which we would not lose, the element which fills our minds whenever we think of our relationship with the one who is our friend? May we not carry this into our thought of man's relation with God? The supreme value of prayer is fellowship with God himself. When we have entered into that fellowship a quiet steals over

the spirit of man. He is not quite so sure of his de-
tailed requests as he was before. His whole outlook
of life begins to change, for he sees things from a new
angle. His life is suffused with new aspirations and
new hopes, and he looks out upon the world with
different convictions than he had before. He makes
requests to be sure, but he is now far more interested
in learning God's will for the world and in praying
that he may be conformed to that will and in giving
his life to proclaiming God's message and helping
others to enter into relationship with him.

When we have learned something about the practice of communion, we begin to enter with God into
his outlook on his world and begin to share his burden
and enter into his joy. The result is that we are
linked with him in all that makes for righteousness
and the bringing in of the kingdom of God. This is
very different from the petty requests and the restless
search for answers to this and that petition which are
to be found among many very good people. And yet,
since prayer is a relation between One who is all-
strong and one who is weak, the element of petition
cannot but play a large part. It is impossible for us
not to make requests of God, that he reach down in
his strength and do for us what we so greatly need
and yet are unable to accomplish in our own strength.

The last question I have to ask in this study is,
What difference does it make to me that I pray for
certain great ends? Is it merely a matter of the lips,
or a pious and not very deeply seated desire? If it
does not make any difference in me, how can I expect
it to make any difference with God? What meaning
is there in the repetition of names and objects when
my interest in these people and objects ends with the

mere mention of them once a day or once a week as they appear on a prayer calendar? There are times when all we can do is to do just that and bring these objects to God and ask him to do what we cannot do, but it is very doubtful whether it reaches the real Christian level, when we are able not only to pray but to do something to bring about the end desired. If prayer does not make a difference in us, causing us to take time and make sacrifices that the ends which are desired may be accomplished, how can we expect God to do that which is necessary to bring these ends to pass? Prayer in a real sense is the bringing of that which we are trying to do and cannot do in our own strength to God, asking his cooperation in that which we so earnestly desire and that on which we are already expending our energy and time and strength. What we need to give careful attention to daily is to keep prayer vital, and prayer cannot be vital unless it causes us to act, unless it makes some real difference in our daily life.

CHAPTER XXI

MUST A MAN BE CONVERTED TO BE A CHRISTIAN?

NOT long ago a candidate for the mission field was asked by a member of the committee examining her whether she could tell another person how to become a Christian. She answered that she would tell that person to do "just the best he could." Was this sufficient? It did not seem so to the committee. Why? I have no doubt this excellent young woman was a Christian, though not a very intelligent Christian. She had very little knowledge concerning the matter which is brought to our attention by the subject of this study. She probably represents hundreds and even thousands who are in the same difficulty. For this reason it is very important for us to attempt to be clear at a point of so great importance.

What ideas are brought to our minds by the term "conversion"? It may be that we think of a very definite experience through which a person passes when he enters the Christian life. It is often thought of as consisting of a very vivid sense of unworthiness and great depression on account of the condition in which one finds himself. It also carries with it the thought of crying to God for forgiveness, and then at the end of a period of agony there comes the peaceful assurance that God has forgiven him and that he is now a child of God. There are many variations in intensity, in inner content, in length of time, and in other features, but I believe it is correct to say that in most cases the feeling element is primary and determines the experience.

Now, the place where the theory becomes questionable is just at the point where the reality of such an experience in the lives of some causes them to claim that it is the necessary experience for all. The tendency is to quote the Scripture passage, "Ye must be born again," and then identify their own peculiar experience with what they suppose was in the mind of Jesus when he used these words. If this identification is complete, the claim easily arises that one cannot be a Christian without just the experience through which many have passed as they have come into the Christian life. Happily, this claim is not made as widely as it once was, with the result that there is far more freedom on the part of Christians with reference to the possibility of coming into the Christian life in a way somewhat different from the way which was traveled by others. But having said this, emphasis must be laid upon the fact that this demand is still carried to a degree almost unthinkable. It is not hearsay with the present writer, but what he has seen and heard and in a real sense been through. He has seen little girls allowed to come to an altar every night, except Saturday night, for three weeks, crying out to God for salvation, a salvation which they were led to think of only in terms of the experience of some older people who had set the type in that community. Such a procedure is absolutely contrary to the facts of psychology and the differing needs of the human spirit. Men have tried to coerce others, to run their experience into a standard mold, and have done incalculable violence to the lives of God's little ones by their insistence.

We must realize, of course, that this tradition has had a long history with many of these typical conversions along the way. Conversions like those of John Bunyan and David Brainerd and many others have been held up as the only way in which men and women and even children are to come out of darkness into light. They have set the type, and the attempt has been made to force all those who would seek after God to find him in some such definite experience. It has created a psychological atmosphere of expectancy which has been powerful in giving direction to the various features of the experience. Thousands of cases have been noted in which this expectancy has either led to certain forms of emotional experience or to very great revulsion, when it has been discovered that such an experience was impossible of attainment to the one who was trying to secure it.

This becomes very evident when such a man as the late Mr. S. H. Hadley, of the Water Street Mission in New York, declares that the men converted there are men who were in youth under the influence of a Christian home environment and training, and that, when they do break away from sin and come into the light of a new life, the form which their experience takes is determined by their boyhood memories and the unconscious influence of many factors which determine how they shall react when they think of religious experience at all. Where this early training is absent the process of becoming a Christian of necessity differs. It is true even in this land where the attempt is made to reach those who have been away from Christian influences and have never known what a real home life was or what it means to pray and read the Scriptures and look to God for guidance in all the crises of life. Even more so does the missionary realize that, when he is dealing with those who have never known anything about Christianity, the approach is determined by the background of tradition and thinking in the community where the man who is thinking of becoming a Christian lives. Of course, it is also determined by the reading of the Bible and the kind of preaching to which he has given attention. But even with these elements, which are the same wherever the Christian gospel is proclaimed, the type of conversion experienced differs according to the individual temperament, the racial background, and the intellectual content of each man who is reached by the gospel.

Let it not be thought for one moment that the question of conversion is either set aside or minimized when certain attitudes toward conversion are condemned, especially when they are held up as a type to which all must conform. We must now turn to the larger questions involved, so that we may realize what conversion may be even in the lives of those for whom a socalled typical conversion is not possible at all.

When we hear a psychologist like Professor James Bissett Pratt say, "In the whole history of ethical discussion there is no saying more full of insight into the nature of the moral life than those words of Jesus, 'Ye must be born again' "[1]—when we hear such declarations we are impressed anew with the very great importance of conversion and realize we must be eager to discover what it really is and ought to be in the life of the church to-day. We must not in any way minimize the experience in Water Street or the Pacific

---

[1] From *The Religious Consciousness*. Reprinted by permission of The Macmillan Company, publishers.

Garden Mission. There we find the "bum," or the "down and out," who, as I have heard Mr. Hadley say, "are so low down that they have to reach up to touch bottom." When these men come to Christ in many cases their conversion is an exceedingly drastic experience, a sudden and complete wrench, and many of the transformations are as wonderful as they are spectacular. Their genuineness and completeness cannot be doubted. These men have become real Christians and they have come into the Christian life through an experience whose validity no one can deny. It is a real type of conversion. Sometimes the insistence that all conversion must conform to this type goes to the extent of thinking that, in order to be typical, a man's experience must include a period of wandering in sin in order that when he turns away from it there may be a very evident and radical recovery through a violent rupture with a life of sin and shame. This is an extreme statement, but I do not believe it is a travesty. The one complete and final answer to be given is to point to tens of thousands of exemplary Christians who have never had such an experience, men and women who could not have passed through such an experience no matter what they might have done to accomplish it. These men and women are just as truly Christians as are others, and we must take account of what has taken place in their lives just as carefully as of the experience of the others.

The question really is concerning two kinds of conversion. The one we have been describing has been looked upon by many as normal, as the type which ought to be looked upon as usual and as most truly respresentative of the way in which a man ought to come into the Christian life. Many Christians at the present time, however, have come to the conclusion that this type of conversion is abnormal instead of being normal. It is not the way in which we should expect and hope that men and women would come into the Christian life. It is for those who have fallen away from rectitude and must be reached, if they are reached at all, through an experience which is terrible yet wonderful. Let us realize that this experience would be normal if we should conclude that everyone must be a hardened sinner before he is a fit subject of conversion and before he can be taken hold of by God and made into a creature fit for his service. We are profoundly thankful that God can work such a change, that he can take a man who has gotten as far away in sin as many have and by a very wonderful work of grace transform him into a character such as we find among those who have been brought out of great darkness and misery into the light of the gospel.

But, thank God, this is not normal, nor should we look upon it as the means by which the vast majority must come into the church. There is another kind of conversion in which one is born again just as truly as through a sudden and cataclysmic experience. It is when a young man or woman in the middle of the adolescent period makes his decision as to what his life shall mean. Until now he has been under authority, but takes the reins in his own hand and makes his own decision for life. It may be very quietly done. He may have led just as good a life morally before as after. It may be he was just as kind in his home and just as thoughtful of others and just as earnest in his studies. The sky to him may have seemed just as blue and the birds may have sung just as sweetly, and yet far down in the depths of his personality he has heard the call of God and makes his decision to put his life into God's hands. Even in these cases there may be a deep consciousness of sin and the turning away from practices and tendencies which are wrong, but the great factor is the realization that a life devoted to God is the only way in which we may do that which will give life its greatest meaning. It is not a spectacular decision. It is usually very quietly reached, but when we see a life of unselfish endeavor flowing from such a decision made quietly during the adolescent years, it is impossible to escape the conclusion that we have here a new creature in Christ Jesus, one whose life is giving evidence of control by the Spirit of God.

We are led to believe that of all the wonderful things which take place in the adolescent period there is none more important than the making of this life decision. As someone has put it, "We make our decisions for sixty when we are sixteen," and then added, "Would that we might make our decisions for sixteen when we are sixty." The first part of this statement, a statement of fact, is correct. The second part, which is a lament, is utterly unfounded. It merely brings into great relief the primary fact that normally we do make the most important decisions for life and character and destiny during these years. It means that the normal form of conversion is just this quiet and in many cases unemotional type. The contrast may not be as glaring, the experience may not be as striking, the change may not be so evident, but, after all, a decision has been made for life and eternity. There is something of finality in the decisions of youth, and very few young men and women change very deeply in their outlook and their purposes after they have made these significant decisions back in the early years of their life. What we should expect, then, of young people is that they should grow up in Christian homes in the nurture and admonition of the Lord. They should always be led to feel that they are God's children, and that, when they take direction of their own thinking and cease to live under the authority of their elders, they should acknowledge God's ownership and devote themselves to him and crave his help in meeting all the situations of life. Whether through a sudden crisis or gradually the change may take place, in every instance its nature is determined by many factors individual and environmental. It makes very little difference so far as these outward features are concerned. The one important question is, Did the young man decide for that which stands in his life for God and character and service?

It seems sad to feel the necessity of making a statement at this point concerning a phrase which has just been used. The theory of many is that until a young person is converted he is not a child of God. How could anyone allow himself to believe such an idea when Jesus took the little children into his arms and said the kingdom of God was made up of people like them? No, our children are children of God as truly as they are children of their parents. It is only by a definite decision against God that they are alienated and separated from him. This happens in many cases but not in all. As young boys and girls come to the age of responsibility at the period when they think for themselves, they do not so much decide for God as if they had been against him, but they decide for God in the sense that they now acknowledge their sonship and desire on their own part to dedicate themselves to him for life and eternity.

Conversion is not a unique phenomenon in Christianity. A recent volume has been published dealing with conversions in various religions in which, with very great differences, the fact becomes apparent that the psychological experiences are very much alike indeed. A number of the great religious leaders of the world have passed through such experiences. Among them may be mentioned Mohammed, the Buddha, Zoroaster, and Saint Paul. The intellectual content in each case differed greatly from that of the others. There is undoubtedly something very distinct in Christian conversion, for here the mind is filled with the revelation of God in Jesus Christ, and that itself is so significant that no other conversions can compare with it when it is true to its highest possibilities. But even in the cases mentioned in other religions there is the same unrest, a struggle, and finally a release when the mind and heart are free and peace comes in to take the place of fear and agitation. There are also differences in intensity and in time and in duration of these experiences. This fact should not be at all disconcerting to Christians as they look upon their own religion and think about it as unique. Were we unable to find any experiences like those through which these men have passed, we would have very much less hope that Christianity could ever win the allegiance of all people everywhere. We are glad men have been converted in other religions, for it gives us assurance that conversion in Christianity will not be strange to their life. Christianity was built for mankind and responds to its needs, the unique feature being that

Christianity is so well fitted to meet these needs that it is able to do for those who are seeking peace and comfort more than any other religion.

And now what is the essence of real Christian conversion? We have had many studies in recent years of the psychology of conversion. Not only are they interesting but exceedingly important, in that they help to determine many things with reference to the process and time and conditions under which we may expect conversion to occur. This assistance was greatly needed. But, after psychology has done all it can do it presents only the human side. There are those who would say that that is all there is to conversion, that it is a subjective experience, that there is no necessity to believe in a God to explain such an experience. But, as Professor Pratt has suggested, if it were not for the conception of God, the psychologists would soon be without material for their science. The first thing about conversion in the estimation of the man who is passing through the experience is that he is dealing with an unseen spiritual Presence which is responsible for all that is taking place. This is the essential element. Without it there might be a continuance for a certain time of an experience through the sheer momentum of tradition, but it would ultimately disappear.

Is there anything more to be said about the content of this experience of the presence of God in the process of conversion? There are so many approaches to the experience that it is very hard indeed to bring the whole matter within the compass of a few statements. Undoubtedly the God who is approached is felt to be so holy that the sinner realizes his unworthiness as he comes into his presence. Thus real conversion is always a morally conditioned relationship. The experience also includes a sense of relief and peace; the rupture between the soul and God is now healed and a relationship of confidence and trust is begun. Peace comes in and takes the place of disturbed unrest. When the experience reaches such a height as that which is exemplified by the apostle Paul it also contains the element of desire for service, "What wilt thou have me to do?" This is as much a part of the experience of conversion as any other if we may judge by what Paul tells us in one of his accounts of what took place on the road to Damascus. In varying degrees these features are present in all conversions which are true to the Christian type. It makes little difference whether there is a deep emotional reaction or not. This has comparatively little to do with it. A man may be exceedingly quiet during the whole experience and yet he is converted. He is converted because, having turned away from his sins or having realized his inadequacy and felt the need of Christ in his life, he comes to him and lays himself before his Lord as the one who is to be the giver of all that which shall fill life with meaning and cause it to be a serviceable life in the years to come. A conversion is to be judged, then, by the effect in life and conduct, and not by the emotional experience through which a man has passed. Has he really come into effective contact with spiritual reality? That is the question whose answer is of supreme importance.

CHAPTER XXII

IS SPIRITUAL MATURITY AN IMPOSSIBLE IDEAL?

WHENEVER the subject of what is known as the higher Christian life is mentioned two questions may be raised, both of which are important. The first is, Is such an experience possible? Paul seemed to think it was. When we read such wonderful passages as are to be found in the fourth chapter of Ephesians our first temptation is to say, "This is too good for men of common clay like ourselves." We are tempted to put away the whole matter, saying that we who live lives in a very rough-and-tumble world cannot be expected to attain what these men and women in Paul's day were given to understand was possible for them. But hold a minute: who were those to whom Paul wrote? With scarcely the possibility of a question the men and women who belonged to the Ephesian and other early Christian churches in the Gentile world were less fitted to receive such a message than we are to-day. They did not have behind them generations and even centuries of Christian tradition and training. Most of them were probably illiterate and were surrounded each day of their lives by a degrading paganism whose atmosphere was one which a Christian could scarcely breathe and still remain pure and noble. We learn from the same chapter in which Paul speaks of full-grown men measuring up to the stature of the fullness of Christ that he was writing to those who had but a short time before been leading very mean and gross lives. We hear him say, "Let him that stole, steal no more." Yes, he was writing to ex-pickpockets and sneak thieves, if not to even more designing burglars. What faith he must have had in the possibilities of the gospel of Christ in human hearts when he could rise to the height of belief in the conversion and the development of such men until they might be filled with all the fullness of Christ! We must be very careful not to measure possibilities by our own poor experience. They should be measured rather by the potentialities of divine grace, which with omnipotent power may work changes in the human heart of which many of us scarcely dream.

But there is another question which is almost as important. Even if such a life be possible, is it desirable? I ask this very seriously, for I am convinced that there are many who feel that to become more spiritual means to become less human, and if we must be dehumanized in order to become spiritual, we shall travel a very short distance in commending our doctrine to noble and high-minded men and women. Is there any real danger? I speak out of deep experience, for I know of those who have refused to take part in the innocent social life of our churches and have refused to attend football games in college because they felt that it was not in accordance with their spiritual profession. We must not hold such men in disdain, men who are living up to the light they have. All I am led to say is that the light they have is a very dim candle indeed. They do not see the meaning of the broader reaches of human life and are not able to appreciate that spirituality is not hindered but may be amplified by all the wholesome and even vigorous relationships of human life. Only the common sense of a deeply spiritual mother saved one young man from going too far in the dehumanizing process in order to obtain what he thought was a spiritual ideal. Since those days there has been attained a different definition as to the relationship which the spiritual must hold to everything that has to do with healthy normal human life.

Coming now more directly to our subject, I am quite sure that in connection with the attainment of a higher religious experience there are one or two misconceptions which must be cleared away before any positive advance can be made. We must take these up before asking ourselves what the steps are in the way toward the higher ideal.

One of the misconceptions is that to attain spiritual maturity means passing through a subjective experience as its distinctive feature, an experience which may be sudden and instantaneous, one which makes a man different from other folks and on the basis of which one ought constantly to be making the profession of perfection. To be sure, there is a real distinction between "perfection in love" and "sinless perfection," but it has not been made sufficiently clear so that a man may not be misunderstood when he speaks of himself as having any kind of perfection. The experience of the present writer is one which very clearly exposes this danger, in that he was led to look for and to profess sinless perfection. It seems almost like blasphemy to him now, but he was sincere at the time, being led to such conclusions by the ardor of those who themselves had made the profession, but without the kind of consideration such a subject demands. It took a long time to become convinced that the attempt to attain an experience as an experience was a real danger. With all the earnestness that he could command at many times for many years he made the attempt to have such an experience and failed. He did not feel any differently in the end than he did in the beginning, until one day he was released as by the breaking of a bond by coming across a book which made very clear to him that an emotional experience was not a necessary factor in the Christian life at all. He was led to see that he would not have to pass through any new experience to have at his disposal all that God had for him. When he was converted he received Christ, and having Christ he had everything that the spiritual life contained for his life and his work. His mind was turned away from his own experiences to the task that God had for him, and he came to realize that the meaning of the Christian life was very far separated from anything that was selfish or self-centered. His eyes were thus being turned away from himself toward Christ and the work he was to do in the world. He was assured that all the power which God had lay at his disposal when he unselfishly gave himself to do that work. From that time on a new life was his, for the simple reason that he was now reaching out after something which was tangible, and before he had been attempting to secure something which one of his temperament could scarcely expect. And, what is more, he learned that the essence of Christianity is unselfishness. While it is necessary to combat self-interest throughout life, it is a great achievement when one begins to turn his eyes away from himself and his own emotional states and look out objectively toward Christ and his task in the world. The important thing in any reaching out after a higher Christian life is the ethical quality, and this is to be interpreted not only as including personal integrity and purity but the ideal of service. When these are prominent in one's mind he has ceased to be primarily interested in the kind of emotional reaction he may have. His anxiety is directed more steadily to what lies before him in work for the Master.

The other misunderstanding concerns the evil nature which each man knows he possesses. Many are still told that this evil nature can be eradicated so that no further solicitations to evil will ever arise in his breast. We must be profoundly thankful to modern psychology for helping us out of this difficulty. We are slowly learning that there are certain ineradicable elements which make up our human nature. We would not be human if we did not have these characteristic marks. They are called instincts. We do not know as much about them as we hope to know when the psychologists have gone further in their task, but what we do know is that an instinct is an inalienable part of our human nature and that we would cease to be human if we lost any one of these essential instincts.

An illustration or two may suffice. A man may have the instinct of pugnacity developed more highly than his fellows. He becomes a Christian, but the instinct of pugnacity is not eradicated. It is there as it was before, but with a very great difference. In his early days he may have been a brawler and a fighter, one who was constantly acting the bully and seeking to have his own way by the sheer might of his strong right arm. He loved to fight, he loved to overcome opposition, but it was all directed by a selfish motive. Now that he is a Christian the old instinct is not absent, but is directed into a new channel and controlled by a new motive. He may be just as great a fighter as he was before, but he now becomes a protector of the weak. He gives himself to the defense of righteousness; he devotes his attention to beating down the attacks of evil men; he is in the arena seeking to bring in the kingdom of God, standing boldly against all those who would make impossible the doing of righteousness in his community. The old instinct is present but is now under perfect control, so that it may even take the form in many cases of passive resistance instead of active opposition. It is the same old instinct as strong as ever, but the entire output of his life is as different from what it was in the old days as day is different from night. Another illustration may be given. Society is dragged down to its lowest depths by misuse of the sexual instinct. If men and women ever come near to hell on earth, it is by a misuse of this God-given power. When used, however, in another direction the contrast is striking. If any man ever tastes the meaning of heaven on earth it is in a Christian home, with wife and children around him and unselfish devotion characterizing the relations in that little circle. Remember, it is precisely the same instinct but now under control, now subdued to a noble purpose, the making of a home, which is doing as much in the world to-day to bring in the kingdom of heaven as all other agencies put together. Let us learn the lesson which is most evident, that in no case is there the eradication of anything fundamental to human nature. If it were eradicated, we would not be men and women, we would be subhuman and could

not attain the heights of Christian experience which
are now open to us. Undoubtedly many have been
led to believe that a certain eradication is possible.
Professor Olin A. Curtis uses a minister as an illustration. This minister has been a very jealous man,
turning green with envy and jealousy when a fellow
minister is praised or given a position higher than
his own. But after having passed through a very
definite experience he never feels jealousy arising
again within him. It is dead, he believes, and dead
forever. This man is in an exceedingly dangerous
condition, Professor Curtis holds, if he is able to per-
suade himself that the account just given is true. For
some time when he does not expect it jealousy will
arise again and he will find himself groveling in the
dust. What we need to remember is that instead of
eradication, the thing to be desired is the redirection
of our instincts, under the control of unselfish ambi-
tion and directed toward constructive ends. This is
what we are to accomplish through our religion, and
this is what the higher Christian life means.

We may now mention as briefly as possible several
of the features which we must consider if we are to
give ourselves to the development of a life which
shall be lived on a level higher than is usual among
professing Christians. In the first place, the foundation of all higher Christian living is moral control. It
is a bitter shame to find men and women making profession of sanctification and yet being no better than
others in their unselfish devotion to children and to
the old folks in the home. It is in these human relationships that we discover to ourselves our attainment or our failure of attainment in the higher reaches
of Christian experience. There must be in the life of

each Christian a certain kind of asceticism. We need to be exceedingly careful at this point. What is usually called asceticism is looked upon as being valuable in itself. I do not have reference to an asceticism of this kind. I do not believe there is any value in abstaining from food merely to abstain, or in being celibate as if there were value in celibacy as such. All these things smack of paganism and elements in Christian history which have not cast off the pagan influence. It contains the unworthy idea of being able to win or help win salvation by such means, "works" Paul called them. What I have reference to is the kind of asceticism which means control of the body in order that the mind and the spirit may be placed first. Paul said that we should keep the body under, not for the sake of keeping the body under, but in order that the body may be compelled to be a servant of the mind and the spirit rather than its master. All indulgences which pamper the body, all practices which make it more difficult for the spirit to assert itself, all those things which may even be innocent in themselves, but which by overindulgence break up the right perspective, are sinful. No one can make any advance in the Christian life, no matter how happy he may feel on occasion or how devoted he is to the church or how much time he spends in devotional exercises, unless he is exercising real self-control. Thus there is danger in indulgence in that the spiritual life suffers because of it. What every man must seek is such a discipline of his life that he shall have a chastened spirit. When he begins to learn the discipline of self-control any possibility of making too bold a profession of perfection is immediately checked. One may rise to the very heavens in an emotional experience, but, if he is not unselfishly serving his fellows and exercising control over his body, it is mere ashes and wind.

Again, becoming spiritually mature means bearing responsibility. It is not so much enjoying religion as promoting it, and this implies that no one can ever hope to attain a higher Christian life whose chief end is not service. This does not mean that the one activity which may be called Christian service is taking part in religious services. We have gotten far beyond that. We actually run the danger sometimes of talking Christianity to death. Our religion now, as it has always been when true to itself, is a life and deeds of service rather than a profession of the lips. Unselfishness in service is an essential mark of spiritual development, and without it there can be no attainment of the higher levels of experience.

In the last place it means a consciousness of spiritual reality. There is, then, a real experience, and there should be much more of it than there is. So frequently there exists a fear of being thought of as peculiar, a kind of satisfaction with mediocrity in religious development. Let us realize, however, that one of the greatest needs of to-day is to make the spiritual world seem real to men and women. There is no greater need in the world to-day. Men and women are living as if there were no spiritual world beyond the vision of the physical eye; they live as if the physical and the material were all. This means the death of ideals and the death of sacrifice for the sake of these ideals. How are men to be persuaded that there is a God and a spiritual world in any other way than by living illustrations of men and women who are in conscious touch with the invisible world and who can make that reality seem tangible to the men and women around them? It can be done only by men and women who are taking time and using energy in order that their own relationship with God shall be kept green and fragrant. They are in daily contact with God and so can take God with them into their daily life. They know the meaning of prayer and therefore can lead others into God's presence. This is the highest value of mature Christian experience, that we are not only sure ourselves of God and of his presence, but are filled with such joy and such peace and are living such consistent lives that men and women are led to desire some of these things which they begin to see in us. Anyone who is able to accomplish this is being sanctified by his contact with God as we see him in Jesus Christ. As in our social life so in our religious life personal contact is the means by which life grows and expands, and there is no other way by which this can be accomplished. This is possible for each of us; it is our privilege and duty.

CHAPTER XXIII

IS THE CHURCH A HUMAN OR A DIVINE INSTITUTION?

WHAT do we mean when we speak of the church? The word is used in a variety of senses. A building may be a church; an assembly of Christian people is spoken of as a church. A group worshiping in a certain building and having a definite organization is a church. A number of such churches bound together by common doctrines and practices, or under a common authority is looked upon as a church. And then very frequently the whole body of Christians in the world is called the church. In view of these different uses it is necessary to seek a meaning which will a little more exactly define what is meant by the church, so that our discussion shall be significant and to the point.

Reduced to its simplest terms, might it not be correct to say that we may speak of a church when any group of people are bound together by their common allegiance to Christ? In Matthew 18. 20 Jesus says, "Where two or three are gathered together in my name, there am I in the midst of them." In essence the church is as simple as that. One might add that the permanence of this group has also come to be an essential factor; it must be a living force through the centuries.

And now after nineteen hundred years of strange and varied history the most important common factor among all the divided branches of the church is just this same feature, that they all profess with equal enthusiasm and earnestness their allegiance to the Lord Jesus Christ. It is impossible to overestimate the significance of this common factor which binds together all those who are sundered from each other and differ in so many ways. Whether he be an adherent of the Orthodox Greek Church or the Roman Catholic or the Anglican or any of the numerous Protestant bodies, with one voice every Christian raises his hands in prayer and adoration to Jesus Christ, the Lord and Master of all.

But so deeply are these different divisions of the Christian Church out of harmony with each other that many have felt that the real Church of Christ is invisible. This invisible church consists of all those in all the branches of the church, and even those on the outside, who are in allegiance to Jesus Christ and thus are bound together in a real, though invisible bond, despite the more or less arbitrary barriers which keep them apart here and now. There are those who would deny the validity of the idea of an invisible church, but what can we say when at the present time the visible organizations of Christendom differ so fundamentally that a Christian who belongs to one cannot belong to another, and yet he realizes that he has Christian brethren far beyond the bounds of his own communion? The nearer he comes to Christ the more truly does he feel the possibility of fellowship with those who in like manner are bound to Christ, though they belong to a different organization and have practices and beliefs which differ in many respects from his own. They are his brethren because of the simple and essential fact that they truly love the Lord Jesus Christ, look upon him as their Saviour, and desire above everything else that his kingdom should come.

But while in essence the church is as simple as it has just been pictured, it was inevitable—yes, inevitable—that as the church grew and spread and as its functions came to be divided, it should assume a definite form. This was necessary to provide for discipline and the propagation of the faith. It developed leaders, and these leaders led the church into definite beliefs and practices, and ultimately into a form of organization, which more or less expressed the genius of the people who were included in its membership, influenced, of course, by the characteristic forms of organization in other lines of activity in the world in which they lived. All these things may not be essential to the idea of the church, but the church could not continue to exist without them. As has already been said, they were inevitable.

The meaning of this must be evident. Human motives and ambitions began to play their part in the history of the church and even more than this, since all kinds of men and women came into these Christian societies, not only human but also sinful motives began to be evident. Looking back over the history of the Christian Church one of the conclusions which cannot be escaped is that as men and women became members of the growing body many brought with them the ideals and practices which paganism had fostered and which were not cast off as they came into the new organization. We may criticize the superficiality of the conversion of these people, but we must remember that whenever large numbers of individuals come rapidly into any new organization it is almost impossible to assimilate them so that their spirit will be identical with the characteristic spirit which was possessed by those who in the early day had caught the true meaning of the faith. The result has been a most checkered story in the course of the long history of the Christian Church.

Is there any way to look back with complacency over this history? The inevitable reaction of any right-minded man is that of deep regret and even indignation that such things should have marred a history which should have been so different. If only more care had been exercised, we find ourselves saying, how many of the mistakes and sins might have been avoided. We may allow ourselves, however, to go too far in this direction. Realizing that human nature is what it is, we cannot and ought not to look for perfection in any institution composed of human beings like ourselves. It is very easy to see that the church is a human institution, very human indeed. It must be such in the very nature of the case. Only when men and women are perfect can we expect perfection in the church of which they are the members.

This being true, what have we the right to look for, since perfection is impossible, in an institution which consists of very human men and women? Is there any possibility of claiming that the church is a divine institution as well as human in view of all the facts which have been presented? If there is anything divine about it, where are we to look for it? How much can we expect of the church if it has a divine element, and by what method can this element be conserved and increased? These are the significant questions which everyone interested in the church is asking to-day.

The answer to which all would agree is that the presence and leadership in the Church of Jesus Christ is the divine element which makes a church truly Christian. It is the first note of any church which calls itself by the name of Jesus Christ. The question is, How can this leadership and presence of Christ be assured in any group of men and women who would seek to justify the application of the name of Christ to the organization to which they belong?

The Roman Catholic Church has a very clear-cut answer to the question. Going back to the statement in Matthew 16: 13–20, the claim is made that the keys of the kingdom of heaven were given to Peter, and that the declaration of Jesus makes Peter the first vicar or representative of himself on earth. Since Peter undoubtedly lived and died in Rome, he is also to be looked upon as the first Bishop of Rome, the first of the long line of the Bishops of that city, who have for centuries been spoken of as Popes. It is not our purpose here to enter into the difficult question of the interpretation of the passage in Matthew on which so many important claims are based. Suffice it to say that the claim of the Church of Rome as stated above is scarcely justified by the best scholarship and cannot be received when it is made to back up all the pretensions of the Church of Rome to unlimited authority over the minds and consciences of men and women everywhere. The right to rule the church they believe was conferred on Peter and upon his successors by virtue of what is known as the apostolic succession. Peter was authorized to transmit the authority and power given him by Christ to his successors by the "laying on of hands"; that is, when Peter laid his hands on the heads of those who were ordained to the ministry, a certain right or power was conveyed upon the ones ordained, and thus through a long succession the authority which was given to Peter was transmitted, until to-day the Pope in Rome claims to speak for Christ and with the authority of Christ in the same way that Peter did through the authority placed in his hands by the word of Christ. The grace of Jesus Christ is thus in their charge and is at their disposal as the representatives of Christ on earth.

This principle determines the nature of the church. It consists of all those who are in communion with the one representative of Christ on earth. To be out of communion with the Roman Bishop, or Pope, is to be out of the church, and hence removed from the relationship with God which brings peace and the assurance of eternal life. Sacramental grace is the means by which the divine power is conveyed to each human being, and there is no other way by which this power can be received. Each priest of the Roman Catholic Church, ordained by a bishop who is in the apostolic succession, is able by the very fact of belonging to that succession to convey that grace to others. It is not contrary to Roman Catholic teaching as interpreted by their own theologians to believe that a priest is not rendered incapable of conveying this grace even though his own life may be full of sin unrepented of and mistakes which he could avoid. If a man desires to be saved, he cannot come to God alone and ask to be restored to his favor on repentance. No, the grace of God cannot reach men in that way. He must come to the church and through the church, which is the channel of divine grace, and receive forgiveness and the assurance of eternal life.

All the other so-called churches are not churches at

all. They are schismatic, separated from God and without the presence of Christ in them. The Romanist is hard put to it to explain how the beautiful fruits of the Spirit are to be accounted for among tens of thousands who are in other churches and out of contact with the "one true church." But theory is stronger than fact, and the Roman Church continues boldly to declare that men and women are eternally lost unless they come to God through the church by way of the sacrament administered by a priest in the apostolic succession. This, however, is very strong doctrine, and a Roman Catholic may take some comfort in the thought which he is permitted to hold that certain individuals out of the church may be saved by the "uncovenanted mercies of God," which may work in the salvation of certain men who through "invincible ignorance" have not been able to see the light, and are thus kept out of the church and away from the grace which can come only through that agency. This means that even Rome is not inflexible, but is compelled to recognize the weight of facts. But it is only a concession. The regular means of salvation is by coming into "mother church." It is exceedingly dangerous to be out of communion with those who have divine grace under their control.

It is quite evident that according to the Roman Catholic theory the church stands between the individual and God, and that man cannot come into contact with God except through that one channel. This intolerable bondage was broken by the Reformation. Martin Luther came to the conclusion that "the just shall live by faith," and that that faith can be exercized irrespective of the ministrations of a priest. A man stands before God alone and can reach up and beseech the forgiveness of God and receive his grace into his heart without the mediation of the church and the ceremonies and ritual and sacraments for which it stands. One of the leading doctrines of the Reformation, a doctrine of which we hear comparatively little to-day, was that of the "priesthood of all believers." According to this doctrine every man has direct access to God. This makes him a priest, since a priest is one who comes into immediate contact with God and is not forced to come into the Divine Presence through any other individual. This was a return to the simplicity of the apostolic period before the days when the Roman Catholic Church had arisen with its claim to absolute sovereignty over the minds and hearts of men.

The Reformation, as can be clearly seen, changed the whole idea of the church, but did not in any sense make any change in what must be looked upon as the essential note of the church, the presence and leadership of Christ. This must be assured if the Christian Church is to exist at all. How, then, can this end be achieved when the church ceases to be a body in which the continued presence of Christ is assured by that means which had been so long recognized in Western Christendom? What could take the place of the apostolic succession, so that we might be sure that Jesus Christ still continued to speak through and to abide in the offices and the ministry of the church? Of all the approaches to this question the only one which is satisfying is that which emphasizes the effective contact of the living Christ with his church through the Holy Spirit. When individual men and women who have felt the touch of Christ transforming their lives join themselves together in their common allegiance to him, in their worship and in the endeavor to carry the gospel to the ends of the earth, we have a true Christian church. The fruits of their life and work confirm their faith that God's living presence is with them, and by these fruits the reality of the claim to be a Christian church is to be judged.

The difficulty with this theory in the minds of many is that it lacks a kind of definiteness which is one of the most agreeable of the features of the Roman Catholic theory. How can we be sure that Christ is present? The Roman priest will tell the inquirer that Christ's presence is assured because of the original appointment of Saint Peter, that God's grace in a peculiar manner has been intrusted to his care, and that by the grace of ordination down through the centuries this same presence has been transmitted and is now just as effective and real in the life of the church as at any time in the past. The Protestant comes in with the question, What shall we say to this claim, when the fruits of the Spirit are manifestly absent? When corrupt Popes and equally corrupt bishops and clergy have caused good men and women to turn their faces away with mingled indignation and grief? The only answer which is possible to make is that the theory breaks down, that we cannot assume that the Spirit of God is present when the fruits of his operation in the hearts of men and women are absent. One of the most significant of all the words of Jesus is when he declares, "By their fruits ye shall know them." This is the key to the Protestant position. Whenever any group of men calling upon the name of Christ and seeking to make him known in the world begin to evidence the fact that Christ is with them through blameless lives and purity of purpose and earnest endeavor to proclaim his name everywhere, we have a church just as really as if Christ himself appeared in person and declared that they were his disciples and that he was with them as they worshiped and sought to proclaim his name.

What about the organization of the Christian Church? Is there just one form which is orthodox and to which all must conform? This is the theory of the Roman Catholic Church, but even in this church we find provision for some kind of development. When John Henry Newman was considering the question of the church and his relationship to it, he tells us that he failed to find the note of "apostolicity"; that is, he found that the Roman Church in his day did not have the precise form which the church of the early apostles exemplified. He tells us in addition that when he could not find this "note" in the church, he discovered that there was another which proved far more important in his thinking. It was the note of "catholicity," according to which the church, to be a true Christian church, must be able at all times and in every place to meet the actual needs of men as those needs arose. In his view the Roman Catholic Church was the only exponent of this idea of catholicity. There are those among Protestants who claim that their church is an apostolic church, a church which is modeled upon the forms and practices and beliefs of the church of the first century. There must surely be a blind spot in the eyes of any who seriously make this claim. Very little study makes it clear that no church at the present time conforms exactly to the type which existed in the apostolic age. There can be no doubt that whether we desire it or not the form of organization will be adapted to the growing and changing needs as they arise from time to time. No form of organization now existent is in any real sense apostolic, nor can it be. What is necessary is that the spirit of the apostolic church be retained, a spirit whose chief inspiration was Jesus Christ and which emphasized his presence in their life and activity. This spirit, expressed according to the needs of each age, is the essential characteristic or note which is to be guarded with great care, for it is at this point that a church proves itself to be a real Christian church or one that may call upon the name of the Master but not realize his presence.

The question of the doctrines of the church, the beliefs and truths which men and women are asked to accept, is exceedingly important and very troublesome in these days. Is it possible to hand down through the ages a set of doctrines formulated with minute care which shall be as acceptable to the twentieth century as they were in the sixteenth or the thirteenth, the fourth or the first Christian century? We need only study the history of the development of Christian doctrine to realize how different the doctrines of one age are from those of another. We are perplexed until we realize that our approach must be from an entirely different angle. We must begin where the New Testament itself began, not with a rigid body of doctrine but with a vital experience of the living Christ. All the doctrines the Christian Church has developed, insofar as they represent vital Christianity, are an attempt to formulate according to the thought forms of the day the meaning of this experience in the human heart. We have a duty laid upon us, just as men had in former ages, of seeing to it that our religious experience is commended to the thinking of intelligent men and women by being expressed in the forms of thought with which they are familiar. They ought also to be forms which are inevitable and which they use naturally when they try to express the deeper facts of life and its relationships and their attitude toward the invisible world. What we should be solicitous about is that, when the Christian religion is presented to men and women, it should be done so clearly and so simply that when they receive these truths the typical Christian experience which has been the same down through the centuries may again be produced. The great necessity resting upon the church is that we may see reproduced through the years renewed expressions of the same spirit, a repetition of the same experience in others which has been the typical expression of Christianity from the beginning until now. Without going into details, it would seem that the only creed necessary to be accepted by everyone coming into the Christian Church is just that creed which will surely make possible the building up of a Christian experience in the lives of men and women. This does not mean that all the elements of Christian teaching are to be included in it. There are many things which are bound up as implications in the Christian way of looking at life, but they need not be included in a working creed. Only those features which are essential to start a person off in the right direction with Christ in his heart and with the hope of a new life coming from that contact are necessary as the creed of any church.

Summing up what has been said, the church is a

divine institution insofar as its life is dominated by the spirit and principles and personality of the living Christ. It is a human institution to be sure, but just as individuals may have their lives transformed by the presence of Christ, so groups of individuals organized in churches may have that really human institution so charged with the same spirit which possesses the lives of the individuals that we may speak of it as a human institution dominated by the Divine Spirit, which is Christ himself working in the hearts of men to-day. It may vary greatly in different places and in different times, just as the Christian experience is very different in one man as contrasted with another, but the essential element which makes a Christian church Christian is that Christ is there more and more dominating the lives of the community which is known by his name.

Is there such a thing as "The Church"? Is there a church par excellence, one which has the right to say, "We are the true church and all who are not in conformity with us are outsiders and aliens"? In one sense an affirmative answer is necessary. That church consists of all those who are united by a common loyalty to Christ and ought to be united in the great common task and it may be in other ways such as worship and belief and polity. Such a church, however, does not exist to-day, and no denomination or any great branch of the Christian Church has such a monopoly upon the Spirit of Christ that it can point the finger of scorn at others and say that they are not churches in as real a sense as they are themselves. We doubtless all agree that such a union should take place among Christian people, now so unfortunately divided and separated that they do not know what a

real "communion of saints" would be like. But so
long as men differ and differ honestly we must remember that it would be most unchristian to attempt to
coerce the belief and the actions of those who differ
from us. This has been attempted many times over
and the result has been only defeat and the opening
of wounds and the loss of the very unity of spirit
which is desired in the process. As soon as coercion
is used something more precious than unity is lost, that
spirit of independence and of the right to worship God
according to the dictates of our own conscience, which
is one of the glories of true Christianity down through
the ages.

But even where coercion is not thought of we shall
all agree that a dead, dull uniformity would be even
worse than the dismembered condition of the churches
to-day. What everyone desires is such a unity that
shall allow for liberty and freedom in organization,
ritual, belief, and emotional expression. What is
coming to be believed by many men whose passion is
the unity of the Christian Church is that this liberty
and freedom would in no essential sense be broken by
differences within the Christian Church, provided the
fundamental loyalty to Christ and the beliefs essentially implied in it shall be the light and guide of all
the branches of the church. When such a union shall
come it must be that of inner cohesion and not of
outward authority. There must be the recognition
that corporate existence is absolutely essential, but
that it exists not for itself but for the proving of the
saints; and when saints differ, as they always have
and always will differ from one another, it is not to be
expected that one form of organization or one type of
emotional expression will prevail. What is necessary

is to make possible the expansion of the kingdom of God among men in such form or forms as shall result in the conversion of men and women, building them up in Christ Jesus, and sending them out equipped to do the work of Christ in the world. When we have that we are in the presence of the Christian Church—and, again let it be said, for the reason that Christ himself is present through his Spirit.

CHAPTER XXIV

IS THE KINGDOM OF GOD AN IMPOSSIBLE DREAM?

WHAT are we as Christians working for? What is to be the final outcome of what we are doing for God in the church? I suppose we all would agree that there is to be set up on earth a kingdom, or a reign of God among men. Doctor James Moffatt in his New Translation of the New Testament prefers to use the word "Realm" instead of "Kingdom," the idea to be expressed being that God's rule is not so much a matter of geography as it is a matter of the condition of men's hearts. Where God rules over the wills of men, so that they are his obedient children, his kingdom has come, at least into their hearts. But the phrase, "the kingdom of God," carries with it the thought that there will be set up on earth a rule of God over the hearts of men which shall be very much more widely established than is true of the Christian Church at the present time. We must be careful not to confuse the kingdom of God on earth with the final heavenly kingdom into which all his children shall finally be garnered. In the ages to come, after the earth as we know it has ceased to be the scene of human activities, we shall continue to live the lives of the blessed in that paradise or heaven which has been prepared for those who love Him. In all probability there would be quite general agreement, except on minor points, on what has just been presented. But from this point on there is marked disagreement as to the nature of the Kingdom and the time and method of its inauguration.

The question is a very difficult one and is not made more easy by the study of the New Testament. What we discover in these writings of the early disciples of Jesus is that they looked for a speedy return of Jesus Christ, even in their own lifetime, who would break down all opposition and rule not merely over the hearts but physically over mankind as a whole, wielding his scepter from the ancient center of the Jewish nation in Jerusalem. It is not possible to get away from the fact that Paul himself held this view. It is quite true that in his later letters there is less emphasis upon the coming of Jesus in the flesh at an early date and a greater emphasis upon the thought of our going out of this world to be with Christ in the heavenly kingdom, but undoubtedly the impression one gets by a careful study of Paul's writings is that he thought that Jesus Christ would return soon, so soon that it was wise for men and women if they were unmarried to remain in that state, because the time would be so short that it would be better not to enter into new relationships and encumber oneself with new duties and responsibilities. It is not possible here to go into a study of all the evidence, but undoubtedly the statement that has just been made is true. If it be true, a very serious conclusion must be drawn, for Jesus Christ did not come back in the sense in which we are led to look upon that coming in the writings of the early disciples and especially of Paul.

This is hard enough when one is trying to interpret the Bible and to see what it actually means for us to-day, but what has been said concerning Paul and the other disciples is not so disconcerting as what we discover in the sayings of Jesus himself. Here we are in difficulty, a difficulty which still remains an unsolved problem in the study of the life of Christ. A very great change, however, is taking place in the minds of the best scholars with reference to this aspect of Jesus' expectation and teaching. If we go back fifteen or twenty years to such a volume as Doctor Albert Schweitzer's *The Quest of the Historical Jesus*, the apocalyptic element fills the horizon almost entirely. Jesus had no other expectation than that he would return soon and be revealed as the heralded Messiah, but he was mistaken, he was a deluded enthusiast. His ethical teaching was meant to apply only during the short period between his ascension and the few years before he would return and rule over the whole world in majesty and power. When we turn to the scholars of to-day we find that this attitude is repudiated, not completely but so effectively that the whole apocalyptic element is being placed in a secondary position among the factors which we must estimate in coming to conclusions concerning what Jesus said and meant. There are so many sayings of Jesus in which the shortened time perspective plays no part that scholars are led to believe that these statements go more nearly to the center of Jesus' teaching and that the apocalyptic sayings are to be interpreted in their light, rather than the other way round. Jesus' own words were put into writing just at the time when his speedy return was being looked for and by those who shared this belief. How much did this influence them in reporting Jesus' words? We have at least one helpful hint. When we take up the Gospel of John, one of the latest of all the New Testament books, we are in a very different situation. Here we find an interpretation in which the Christ of the eternities is unveiled and in which all thought of a speedy return in the flesh seems to have been superseded by those features of Jesus' teaching which reach out through the years and connect themselves with the eternal purposes of God.

All through the Christian centuries there have been those who felt the fascination of the imminent coming of Christ and have made very much of it. One of the earliest heresies which disrupted the church in certain quarters and which even led astray so great a Christian as Tertullian was Montanism, which started in the central part of Asia Minor among the violently enthusiastic men and even more irrepressible women of those parts and spread fairly widely over the Christian Church of the third century. This movement claimed that spiritual gifts were available then as they were in the apostolic period, and that Christ would return in the immediate future and restore the fellowship with himself which the disciples of Jesus themselves enjoyed. The sobriety of the leadership of the church, however, curbed the enthusiasm of these more or less deluded and one-sided followers of Jesus and led the church into a saner attitude toward life and its relationship to the future.

It is impossible to trace the history of the whole movement, but it may be of interest to call attention to Martin Luther, whose mind was strongly tinctured with the belief that in his day the end of the world was near at hand, when Jesus Christ would come in his might and put an end to everything which was then taking place. Luther even used this expectation as an argument against the carrying of the gospel to the heathen nations. He makes the explicit statement that there was not time enough left to perform so great a task as to take the message of Jesus to the nations of the world, when he felt sure that Jesus would return in so short a time.

Going back over the history of the Christian Church, it becomes evident that there has always been a recrudescence of these views whenever persecution has arisen or some great world tragedy like the recent World War was being enacted. We have been in the midst of such a rebirth of intense devotion to the ideas of Christ's speedy return and the coming of the Kingdom through his presence on earth, so that a great many men and women have been caused to be deeply troubled over the interpretation of Christianity which is implied in this view. Unfortunately, the theory is held with such intensity that it tends to separate Christians who hold the theory from others. It divides churches and makes it difficult if not impossible for Christians who differ in their interpretation at this point to have fellowship in worship and in service. The cleavage has extended to the mission field and both among native Christians and missionaries there have been those who have arrayed themselves on one side or another and have almost gone to the extent of anathematizing those who do not agree with them in every detail.

We ought to understand if possible how such serious results can follow the acceptance or the denial of such a theory as this. Those who believe in the imminent coming of Jesus Christ, who believe that his coming will be before the millennium, which can only be brought about by his coming, are called Premillennialists. They are usually very literal in their interpretation of the Bible, demanding implicit acceptance of the statements which are made because, as they hold, every word, even every letter, is the result of direct inspiration, and so must be accepted just as it stands with no question. They are very strenuous in upholding the absolute inerrancy of each statement of the Bible and supporting with great vigor the authority of the whole Bible on every question with which it deals, whether it be moral and religious or scientific and historical. By a minute study of the Bible, without consideration in many cases of the relationship of one passage to another, they have worked out a "scheme of the ages," elaborate and complex, which purports to tell what has happened, is happening, and will happen, from the beginning of time until the ushering in of the final period when time shall be no more. They have fashioned a philosophy of history and of Christianity so complete and watertight, with every part having its appropriate and necessary place, that one cannot touch or question any part of it without disturbing the whole structure.

According to this scheme Jesus Christ left his disciples with the promise (Acts 1. 10f.) that he would return. We are living then in the interval between his departure and his coming again. The purpose of this interval in the mind of God is to give opportunity to preach the gospel over the whole world, in order to gather out from the nations those whom God has chosen, in other words the elect, or as it is put in the book of Revelation, the 144,000 "sealed ones." When this has been accomplished, this period or interval will be closed and Jesus Christ will come back with

might and power to put an end to the world as we
know it to-day.

There is some difference among these Premillennialists as to the exact "times and seasons," but for prac-
tically all of them the signs now point to his speedy
coming. The end cannot be long delayed, so they
say. When Jesus returns, which is called his Parousia,
or Presence, the Jews as a whole will be converted to
the Christian faith, Jesus will set up his rule in Jerusalem, the dead in Christ shall arise from their graves
and join the living believers, the unbelieving nations
will be defeated and crushed and Christ will reign
with his saints on this earth a thousand years, which
is known as the millennium. After that there will be
a short period when the hosts of darkness shall be
liberated, and after that shall go down in utter defeat,
and finally there will be the Judgment before the great
white throne, the separation of the good from the evil,
and the paradise of heaven for the saints forever in
eternal bliss. Undoubtedly, the exact order may be
stated differently by different teachers, and more emphasis may be placed on one point than another by
this or that school, but, roughly, this is the idea which
is conveyed by the teaching of those who hold that the
kingdom of God cannot come until Jesus returns and
brings it in by his omnipotent power.

What part are we as Christians to play in all this?
Our work is to preach faithfully the gospel of Christ
and thus help gather out the elect whom God has
chosen and whom he knows in every country in the
world. But are we not to do more? Are we not to
make this a better world, a fit place for men and
women and girls and boys to live in? Of course it is
admitted that wherever Christians are they will seek

to better the conditions around them, but this is entirely secondary, even negligible in the estimation of those who propound these views. No, this is a perfectly hopeless world, which is going from bad to worse. Nothing we can do will hinder or effectually restrain the growing degeneracy. The wickedness of the age is to them one of the most evident signs of the rapidly approaching end of the world. Only the chosen ones will be able to escape the awful destruction which will ensue when Jesus Christ comes back in power. We must give credit to those who hold these views for being in many cases devoted followers of Jesus who seek to lead noble lives and who shed the influence of their religion upon all those with whom they come in contact. It would be utterly unfair not to make clear that some of the very best men and women now living are those who hold this theory and who are trying faithfully to do as they believe the Bible commands.

But when this has been said, we are compelled to ask some very pertinent questions concerning the theory itself. Can we accept it even though good men may proclaim it? These men claim to have Scripture with them, but it is very hard to understand how Scripture can be looked upon as justifying their view of a speedy return of Christ at the present time when the promise of a speedy return was made nineteen hundred years ago. Scripture is surely not with them at this crucial point. If the literal statements we find in the Bible were true when they were written, they cannot be true to-day, for the word "soon" when written nineteen hundred years ago could not be stretched out and expanded to bring the year 1926 within its scope. There is another approach which is necessary if we would save the Bible from this kind of ill treatment, and at the same time allow it to speak out its age-long lessons to our hearts.

The time element in prophecy is exceedingly important and needs to be understood. George Adam Smith compares it to a mountain range. Seeing the mountains from a distance they appear one solid mass, beautifully tinted in purple and lavender. When one comes closer he begins to realize that it is not one mass, but is broken up into ranges, which are superimposed, one upon another, with deep valleys in between, the farthest range being much farther off than he dreamed of when he first saw the mountains over the horizon. When the traveler approaches the very foot of the mountains many details which he had not seen even at a relatively nearer approach become visible. He sees that there are streams and waterfalls, that there are trees and woods here and there which could not be seen until the mountains are actually entered and one finds himself in a perfect maze of hills and valleys, crags and torrents, forests and snowfields, none of which could be seen from the far distance. The mountains have become a very different place now that he is actually in close contact with them. What George Adam Smith means is that, no matter how clearly a seer may be able to hold up a future prospect, it never is just the same when he looks at it from the distance as it is when one comes into very close contact with it. What we discover in Old Testament prophecy is the conviction that some great event is to take place, but there is what has been called the foreshortening of perspective, so that the intervening distances between events do not appear at all. All the seer sees is an important event;

what he fails to see is the effect of time as it changes the perspective upon the approach of the event through the years. This takes place whenever in the Bible some great future event is foreseen. There seems to be a loss of the sense of time, and the seer speaks of the wonder and the terribleness of that which he believes is immediately before him. The Jewish people were led to believe that a Messiah was coming, but it would be impossible to write a life of Christ from the Old Testament references to the Coming One. The fulfillment is necessary to interpret the prophecy as much as the prophecy was necessary to create the impression of a great day coming.

Not only the imagery but even the words of the apocalyptic discourses in the New Testament are taken from other and older apocalyptic writings which are not to be found within the canon of our Scriptures. This indicates that the biblical writers used as their literary vehicle a well-known current form much used in that time. We find it exceedingly difficult to attach a literal interpretation to the elaborate visions of these discourses. What scholars have come to feel is that there is much that is the mere trappings of the truth and not the eternal truth itself. What is needed is the careful study which will result in giving us the essential message which is eternal in the midst of a form which had significance only for the men and women of the time in which these writings were originally read. Again, we must be very careful not to make the mistake of thinking that prophecy is "history written beforehand." As Doctor Charles Hodge, of Princeton, said many years ago, the purpose of prophecy is not to write history beforehand, but to create a moral impression. Our duty is to dig down underneath and find out the inner meaning Jesus had in mind and to discover in the midst of discourses which contained much that was local and temporary that which is of abiding significance.

It is impossible in a study like this to go into detail, but I believe that with assurance it is possible to say that throughout these writings one thing is evident, that all that is and all that is to take place in the future is under the control and direction of the living Christ. He is present, though unseen, in all that happens and in all we do. As his followers we are bound to proclaim him as the one hope of man and society, with the calm assurance in our hearts that in the end the consummation of all will be in his hands as it was in its inauguration. He is the finisher as well as the author of our faith. We have his promise that he will be with us to the end of the world. This is as near a statement of the abiding truth in all these statements that students feel they are justified in making to-day.

But what are we to do with the many statements concerning the return of Jesus and the millennium? Is not everything essential provided for in the statement already made? When we have sifted out all that is local and applicable to a distant time in the past, the great fact remains that Jesus Christ is our living Lord, that he is with us to-day, and that he is to reign until all enemies are put under his feet. Jesus Christ is the Judge. There is to be a distinction made between the destiny of the righteous and the evil and there is to be a final consummation when God will be all in all and the blessedness of the eternities will be

ushered in. Let us be very sure that the presence of
Christ now is a reality and that his Spirit is actually
at work in the world to-day. All the results toward
higher ideals and a deeper righteousness come from
him through that Spirit which is at work in men's
hearts everywhere.

In view of the work of God in human society to-day,
what is our duty? Should we not here as elsewhere
go back to Jesus Christ and try to follow in his steps?
What did he do as we follow him through his brief life
of activity in Galilee and in Jerusalem? We find him
meeting every need, physical and mental as well as
moral and spiritual. He seemed to make no difference
between the needs as they arose. Wherever a man or
woman or child needed his ministry, his great heart
of compassion went out and began to give of itself,
that healing and strength might come. This is what
we should do. Individual needs must be met, but so
must the burning needs of human society. As he
met the needs of the body, so must we; as he healed
the sickness of the soul, so must we do our part in
the cure of those who are sick in sin. This same compassion should lead us, whenever the relations of man
in society result in suffering and disgrace, to give
ourselves that these relations may be ameliorated and
men may become more nearly brothers the world
around. How can we doubt that in this present day
Jesus Christ stands near at hand by the side of those
who would bring about better international relationships, with the great end in view that wars may cease
and that he may indeed be crowned the Prince of
Peace?

What shall we say in answer to those who would
declare that all this is useless, that the world is grow-

ing worse, that nothing can come but evil out of the tendencies now at work in human society? It is very true that in short perspective there are times of real retrogression, but if we take a sweep of five hundred years or a thousand years or four thousand years, it becomes amply evident that men have learned many things, one of which is how to live together with more consideration for others than was true in times past. This can be said with even the Great War staring us in the face and the bitter hatreds of the years that have followed. God's Spirit is in human society putting new ideals of peace and brotherhood into the minds of men and making them look forward to the actual dominance of these principles. This is a hope which men have had for long years, but never with the confident expectation which now possesses the breasts of an increasing number of the best and wisest of the men and women in the world.

One other question may be asked: Is the final consummation of all things to be in this world? Let me quote from Doctor Walter Rauschenbusch, one of the great apostles of the social gospel of our times: "In asking for faith in the possibility of a new social order we ask for no Utopian delusion. We know well that there is no perfection for man in this life: there is only growth toward perfection. . . . We shall never have a perfect social life, yet we must seek it with faith. We shall never abolish suffering. There will always be death and the empty chair and heart. There will always be the agony of love unreturned. Women will long for children and never press baby lips to their breast. Men will long for fame and miss it. Imperfect moral insight will work hurt in the best conceivable social order. . . . At best there is always but an approximation to a perfect social order. The kingdom of God is always but coming."[1]

Jesus shall rule the hearts of men here in this world, but we shall not find complete satisfaction. There will always be an aching void, there will always be a desire for something more, so that we shall be compelled to look forward to that consummation in the eternities when we shall be like him, when we shall see him as he is, and when all the heartaches of this present life shall cease to be, and when there shall be such a reunion of the spirits of the blessed under conditions which can never be attained here in this world. There must come a day when tears and sorrow shall be no more, and that can never be under earthly conditions. But thank God there is a heaven where all our dreams shall come true and where the best is held in readiness for those who can appreciate it.

---

[1] From *Christianity and the Social Crisis*. Reprinted by permission of The Macmillan Company, publishers.

CHAPTER XXV

IS CHRISTIANITY THE FINAL RELIGION?

JOHN the Baptist, in the discouragement which came to him in prison, sent his disciples to ask Jesus, "Art thou he that should come, or look we for another?" (Luke 7. 19-23.) The same question is now being asked again, only it is put in this form: Is Christianity God's final word to men, or is it merely the best religion up to the present time? The question is an exceedingly pertinent one and demands far more consideration than Christians have given it. To say that it is difficult should not make us less willing to deal with it if the question itself is important.

I suppose that most Christians implicitly and by a kind of intuition do look upon their religion as not only the best word up to the present but the final word, not to be superseded. If, however, this naive faith is to become a deep and intelligent conviction, articulated with all the other factors which enter into the mental equipment of the modern man, it can only be done by setting oneself to the task and seeing it through. For just as soon as one makes the statement that Christianity is the final religion he is confronted with real difficulties, and the only thing to do is to face them unflinchingly.

What right has anyone to make such an assertion when he really does not know anything about the future? Christianity, we are told, may be the best religion in the world to-day but, just as Christianity arose to meet a need, other needs may arise at some future time which will demand some new religion, which shall do for that day what Christianity is doing now. What would be more natural than to believe that just this thing not only might happen but, judging by the past, is the most likely thing that could happen? Surely, it would be most unscientific to attempt to say now what is to happen or is not to happen in the course of human development. Who knows what man may become and what needs he may develop, needs which could only be satisfied by means which are as impossible of discovery now as the needs themselves are of being imagined? I am of the opinion that this weighty consideration needs to be put as strongly and clearly as possible. For the one tremendous fact lying back of the ideas expressed in it is that we do not know what is to occur in the future, and therefore we should be exceedingly careful about making any predictions concerning what may take place in the years to come.

There is still another line of reasoning to which recourse may be had, to strengthen the doubt as to whether we have any right to declare that Christianity is to be the religion of the final phases of human life among men. The doctrine of evolution lends its powerful aid to any disparagement of predictions concerning the future. The earth is still developing and so are man and society. It is of their very genius to change from the more simple to the more complex, to assume new forms, and who can say exactly what the end shall be? Anyone who has taken the time to study the history of religion will realize that it too has developed and is developing to-day. Accordingly, is it not the height of absurdity

to make the claim that what we now have is what
must be the religion of the ages to come? Again I
do not wish to minimize in any way the force of this
argument.

I think enough has been said to indicate both the
direction and the strength of the considerations which
have been raised against the finality of Christianity.
I feel the force of this argument as keenly as any, and
I will go as far as to say that there can be no scientific
method of disproving the contention. The argument
cannot be disproved, using proof of course in the
strict sense. But let us realize that the argument we
are using is about as long as it is short; that if science
cannot prove the finality of Christianity, it cannot
disprove it either. If we do not know the future, let
us realize that we have no more right to say that
Christianity cannot be the religion of the ages to come
than we have of saying that it must be. What we are
coming to is the thought that our scientific instruments fail to measure and weigh the kind of considerations necessary to deal with such a question. If
we are able to believe that Christianity is the final
religion, it will not be because we are led to do so by
scientific investigation. If, on the other hand, we
come to the conclusion that Christianity cannot be
the final religion, we must remember that it is not
because science led us to that conclusion. All that
science can do is to warn us against a certain over-
confidence, which may possess the minds of men and
leave us in a position open to easy attack. Even an
evolutionist, if he realizes the limitations of his theory,
cannot determine the nature of the development in the
time to come; so that if we are to arrive at any conclusion at all, it must be by some other approach than

that which the scientist as a scientist is able to put into our hands.

When we speak about the claim of Christianity to be final it is necessary to distinguish carefully exactly what is meant. There are many things connected with Christianity which no one would want to think of as final; that is, no one who has an appreciation of the ideals which we are working for as contrasted with the actualities of the past and the present. No one who thinks deeply can believe that the organization of the church, its form, its experience, its theology, will always be just what they are to-day. All of these have changed in the past, are changing to-day, and must continue to do so. We must remember, however, that in touching these questions we have not yet come into contact with that which is essential to Christianity, the vital center of the faith. The ultimate fact is that in Jesus Christ we have a real revelation of God, that we know what the final fact of the universe is like, that we are intelligently in touch with ultimate Reality. Christianity asserts that this is true, and that being true it is a final, unalterable fact, and therefore it is the absolute, the final religion. God is the great unchanging fact of the universe, who causes it to be what it is. When once we have seen him we have had a glimpse of something that is final as well as real. As Professor Mackintosh puts it, "By affirming the 'absoluteness' of Christianity we mean that in dealing with Jesus we are dealing with God himself."[1]

Having made these statements as clearly as possible, we come now to ask the question directly, What

---

[1] Reprinted by permission of Charles Scribner's Sons, publishers.

right has a Christian to assert the finality of his faith? Let us remember that implicitly or explicitly Christians have always made this claim. The author of the book of Hebrews puts it in classic form: "Jesus Christ *is* the same yesterday and to-day, *yea* and forever" (Heb. 13. 8). The serious question arises whether to-day or at any time the faith would not loosen its grip upon its followers unless they could hold to this feature of finality. And yet every Christian who thinks is compelled to ask why it may not happen that some great crisis might make necessary a complete reconstruction of what man has looked upon as essential in his religious attitudes and thought. But with all this, does it not become quite evident that if Christ is not the very image of the invisible God, the question is one not only of the future but of the present, that is, we may be mistaken now and may be only groping in imperfect light, not even possessing the deepest truth to-day?

As a matter of fact, one who has been captured by Christ has no misgivings about the future. It is not difficult for him to believe that Christ has the element of finality about him, and that in the ages to come it will be the same Jesus with whom he now has to do who will be his Lord in the heaven to be. It is the man who is doubtful about his religion to-day who is likely to be uncertain about the future. The best illustration I know is that of human marriage. It is only the man who is not sure of his love now who feels he might meet some other woman who would mean more than his present wife or fiancee. He who is really in love has no misgivings for the present or the future. There is a kind of finality about true human love which carries with it a peace not only for the present but as one peers down through the years. The analogy is not perfect but it is exceedingly suggestive, and is something akin to the finality which characterizes a man's relationship with Christ. The lover is anchored now and has no misgivings about the future. So it is with the man who is truly in love with Christ and has been captured by him. He may not be able to prove it by scientific methods any more than the lover can, but he is held by a conviction so deep that he is willing to risk everything in life and in the future on his faith that what is now will remain essentially unaltered down through the years.

After all, it is the ability of Christianity to meet a given situation which gives the assurance that it can meet any other situation. Just as we are completely satisfied to-day so we shall remain satisfied in the future—that is, if our natures have been touched to their very core. This is true of human love, and it is true of the relationship of the human soul and God as he is revealed in Christ. But the evolutionist might come in at this point and say that some new situation might arise which is utterly dissimilar to anything we now know, and once in a while an ardent and superficial evolutionist will arise and say that that is just what is likely to happen. We must be exceedingly cautious here and listen to what the wiser evolutionists say. The past is not a dead past but lives in the sense that it teaches us lessons which actually reveal realities in our experience to-day. The fact which is exceedingly clear is that evolution not only proceeds along lines which we may discover but that it actually arrives at conclusions, reaches limits, and ceases to evolve further. No evolutionist is foolhardy enough to say that a human being will ever develop